WE ARE ALL BLACK

Abhijit Naskar is the twenty-first century scientific mind, whose glorious philosophical touch has enabled modern Neuroscience to effectively engage in the human society towards diminishing the ever-growing conflicts among religions. As an untiring advocate of global harmony and peace, he became a beloved best-selling author all over the world with his very first book "The Art of Neuroscience in Everything". With various of his pioneering ventures into the Neuropsychology of religious sentiments, he has hugely contributed to humanity's attempt of eradicating religious differences, for which he is popularly hailed as a humanitarian who incessantly works towards taking the human civilization in the path of sweet general harmony.

Also by Abhijit Naskar

The Art of Neuroscience in Everything

Your Own Neuron: A Tour of Your Psychic Brain

The God Parasite: Revelation of Neuroscience

The Spirituality Engine

Love Sutra: The Neuroscientific Manual of Love

Homo: A Brief History of Consciousness

Neurosutra: The Abhijit Naskar Collection

Autobiography of God: Biopsy of A Cognitive Reality

Biopsy of Religions: Neuroanalysis towards Universal
Tolerance

Prescription: Treating India's Soul

What is Mind?

In Search of Divinity: Journey to The Kingdom of
Conscience

Love, God & Neurons: Memoir of a scientist who found
himself by getting lost

The Islamophobic Civilization: Voyage of Acceptance

Neurons of Jesus: Mind of A Teacher, Spouse & Thinker

Neurons, Oxygen & Nanak

The Education Decree

Principia Humanitas

The Krishna Cancer

Rowdy Buddha: The First Sapiens

WE ARE ALL
BLACK

A TREATISE ON RACISM

ABHIJIT
NASKAR

We Are All Black: A Treatise on Racism

Copyright © 2017 Abhijit Naskar

This is a work of non-fiction

An Amazon Publishing Company, 1st Edition, 2017

Printed in United States of America

ISBN-13: 978-1545191972

Dedication

To Africa – the Motherland of us all.

CONTENTS

Acknowledgement 1

Chapter I - Our Motherland Africa.................3

Chapter II - Neurobiology of Racism...........60

Chapter III - One Humanity 105

Bibliography 115

ACKNOWLEDGEMENT

A treatise in the domain of science and philosophy, that attempts to make a resolving biological analysis of humanity's one of the most disgraceful characteristic stains, and come up with a civilized means to march ahead in the path of unified progress, can never be the work of one scientist or philosopher. Here, I – Naskar is merely the end product of centuries of rigorous neuroscientific, paleoanthropological, and humanistic endeavors. And the minds that I owe the most in my pursuit of unifying humanity as one species, are as follows.

Leo Tolstoy - the greatest and the most rational Christian that I know of.

Charles Darwin - the greatest scientific product of his time.

Martin Luther King Jr. – the man who redefined what it is like to be human.

Michael A. Persinger – the scientist without whom Naskar would have never met the world of Neuroscience.

Now there was another man, who molded a childish mind into an excessively curious one – his name was Gadadhar Chatterjee. Without this man, I'd have remained a rat in the race. Without this man, Naskar would have never been truly awakened from the deep sleep of ancient ignorance and mysticism. He didn't have even the basic literacy to understand the English alphabets, yet to me he was The Philosopher of All Philosophers, and the Thinker of All Thinkers.

CHAPTER I
Our Motherland Africa

If origin defines race, then we are all Africans –
we are all black. No matter how fascinatingly
white one's skin is, or how classy one's accent
of English is, the fact remains, the whole of
humanity comes from the land of Africa. It is
the cradle of our species. It is the glorious
womb in which we evolved. Biologically
speaking, there is only original race of humans
in this world, and that is African. And once the
whole human population realizes this simple
paleoanthropological fact, there would no
longer remain any such disgraceful
phenomenon as Racism. We all are basically a
little better looking African Apes.

Imagine, a Chinese immigrant couple settles
happily in America. They become American
citizens and eventually have a baby there, who

is technically born and raised as an American citizen. He (could be she too) grows up to be a brilliant physicist at the New York City College. Now, even though this brilliant scientist is hailed by the society, for sociological purposes, as an American citizen, the fact remains, that his origin lies in China. Now turn this into a global phenomenon of the whole species. Every single human being may sociologically be hailed as some sort of national citizen, but the origin of all humans on earth goes back to one specific land – the land of Africa. Thus, in the eye of a genuine human, there is only race that exists in human society, which is the human race. American or not, Canadian or not, Australian or not, Asian or not - before anything else, you are a human first.

Our species Homo sapiens evolved around 200,000 years ago in Africa and then migrated to various corners of the world. Over time the color of the skin began to differ among all those scattered humans, as they started to adapt to their vividly different environmental conditions. Thus, differences in skin color and physique simply reflect adaptation to different environments. It does not get any simpler than this. Saying that some members of humanity are superior to some other members, simply because of the color of their skin, is the same as discriminating between two daughters of the same mother simply because one is blonde and the other is brunette.

If not as a true human, let me tell you as a Biologist, color of the skin does not define an individual's intelligence – it does not define an individual's ambitions - it does not define an individual's dreams – and above all, it does not define an individual's character. It is character that should be the sole measure of judgement in the society of thinking humanity, and nothing short of that would do.

Biologically speaking, we the humans evolved from the same African ancestors that gave rise to the gorilla and the chimpanzee. The gorillas and the chimpanzees can be hailed as lesser species, for all sorts of empirical reasons. Let's just say, the chimpanzees don't even know that they are called chimpanzees, nor the gorillas know that they are termed as gorillas by the humans! This is enough reason for even the lay person to recognize that they are not as superior as the humans. But when a portion of the human population is perceived by their fellow humans as lesser species, it is what makes the perceivers lesser humans.

No Lord Almighty created the humans out of personal will. Creationism is simply a myth created by the weak and ignorant humans out of a psychological need to have a sense of eternal security. We along with all other living organisms on earth evolved over a long period of time. Life itself is around 3.5 billion years old, and in this aspect, the earth is not much older than that, being only about a billion years older. Our planet formed as a hot mass of molten rock about 4.6 billion years ago. As the earth cooled, much of the water vapor present in its atmosphere condensed into liquid water, which accumulated on the surface in chemically rich oceans.

Paige: de-evolution

One scenario for the origin of life is that it originated in this dilute, hot smelly soup of ammonia, formaldehyde, formic acid, cyanide, methane, hydrogen sulfide, and organic hydrocarbons. Whether at the oceans' edge, in hydrothermal deep-sea vents, or elsewhere, the consensus among researchers is that life arose spontaneously from these early waters less than 4 billion years ago. While the way in which this happened still remains a puzzle, one cannot escape a certain curiosity about the earliest steps that eventually led to the origin of all living things on earth, including ourselves. In this case, all we can do is to keep searching and not give in to mystical non-sense, due to our lack of knowledge beyond a certain point. Remember, this threshold of human understanding never remains stagnant, it always keeps moving a step further, turning a little of the unknown into known, bit by bit.

In an attempt to speculate how life might have originated, so far, we scientists have concocted two possible hypotheses. One hypothesis suggests that life may not have originated on earth at all, instead, it may have reached earth from some other planet. This hypothesis is known as the theory of panspermia. Another hypothesis, known as the theory of spontaneous origin, suggests that life evolved spontaneously from inanimate matter, as associations among molecules became more and more complex.

The theory of panspermia proposes that meteors or cosmic dust may have carried significant amounts of complex organic molecules to earth, kicking off the evolution of life. Hundreds of thousands of meteorites and comets are known to have slammed into the early earth, and recent findings suggest that at least some may have carried organic materials.

Most of us scientists tentatively accept the theory of spontaneous origin, that life evolved from inanimate matter. In this view, as changes in molecules increased their stability and caused them to persist longer, these molecules could initiate more and more complex associations, culminating in the evolution of cells around 3.5 billion years ago.

These cells got more and more complex over time and eventually gave rise to the wide array of living creatures on earth, including us humans.

The story of human evolution begins around 65 million years ago, with the explosive radiation of a group of small, arboreal mammals called the Archonta. These primarily insectivorous mammals had large eyes and were most likely nocturnal. Their radiation gave rise to different types of mammals, including bats, tree shrews, and primates, the order of mammals that contains humans.

Primates are mammals with two distinct features that allowed them to succeed in the arboreal (living in trees), insect-eating environment – grasping fingers and toes, and binocular vision. Other mammals have binocular vision too, but only primates have both binocular vision and grasping hands, making them particularly well adapted to their environment. While early primates were mostly insectivorous, their dentition began to change from the shearing, triangular shaped molars specialized for insect eating to the more flattened, square-shaped molars and rodentlike incisors specialized for plant eating. Primates that evolved later also show a continuous reduction in snout length and number of teeth.

About 40 million years ago, the earliest primates split into two groups: the prosimians and the anthropoids. The prosimians ("before monkeys") looked something like a cross between a squirrel and a cat and were common in North America, Europe, Asia, and Africa. Only a few prosimians survive today such as, lemurs, lorises and tarsiers. In addition to having grasping fingers and toes and binocular vision, prosimians have large eyes with increased visual perception. Most prosimians are nocturnal, feeding on fruits, leaves, and flowers, and many lemurs have long tails for balancing.

The higher primates such as monkeys, apes and humans, are known as Anthropoids. Almost of them are diurnal, that is, active during the day, and feeding mainly on fruits and leaves.

Figure1.1 The Tarsier - a prosimian native to tropical Asia, shows the characteristic features of primates: grasping fingers and toes and binocular vision

Evolution through natural selection favored many changes in anthropoid eye design, including color vision, that were adaptations to day-time foraging. Few of the prosimians are also diurnal, and quite like them, the anthropoids live in groups with complex social interactions of their own. Unlike the most of the animal kingdom, the anthropoids tend to care for their young for prolonged periods – this allows for a long childhood of learning and brain development.

About 30 million years ago, some anthropoids migrated from their homeland Africa to South America, where they evolved in isolation. Their descendants, known as the New World monkeys, are quite easy to identify - all are arboreal, they have flat spreading noses, and many of them grasp objects with long prehensile tails. The most significant distinction between the New World and Old World monkeys is found in the tail part. The Old World monkeys lack the prehensile tails that the New World ones have.

Around 25 million years ago, anthropoids that remained in Africa split into two lineages: one gave rise to the Old World monkeys and the other gave rise to the hominoids. Old World monkeys include ground dwelling as well as arboreal species. Their nostrils are close together, their noses point downward, and some have toughened pads of skin for prolonged sitting.

Figure 1.2 New and Old World monkeys. (Left) New World monkeys, such as this golden lion tamarin, are arboreal, and many have prehensile tails. (Right) Old World monkeys lack prehensile tails, and many are ground dwellers.

The Apes or Hominoids is the African anthropoid lineage to which belong the gibbons (lesser apes) and the hominids. The lesser apes, i.e. the family Hylobatidae, consist a total of sixteen species. The Hominids on the other hand consist of the orangutan (Pongo), gorilla (Gorilla), chimpanzee (Pan) and us the humans and our direct ancestors (such as Australopithecines and others). Hominids are also called Great Apes.

Figure 1.3 The living apes other than humans. (a) Mueller gibbon, Hylobates muelleri. (b) Orangutan, Pongo pygmaeus. (c) Gorilla, Gorilla gorilla. (d) Chimpanzee, Pan troglodytes.

Apes have larger brains than monkeys, and they lack tails. With the exception of the lesser apes, i.e. the gibbons, which is small, all living apes are larger than any monkey. Apes exhibit the most adaptable behavior of any mammal. So, we humans are quite literally apes as well. And among all other living apes, chimpanzees are our closest relatives. Fossil records along with studies of human and other ape DNA, reveal that we the humans shared a common ancestor with chimpanzees and bonobos sometime around 6 million years ago.

Now, let's have a closer look at the evolution of our species in Africa, from near the end of the geological time period known as the Miocene, just before our lineage diverged from that of chimpanzees and bonobos. After this split all the members of our side of the hominid tree are known as Hominins. Hominins include us the humans and all our direct ancestor species. As revealed by fossil records, bipedal walking and smaller, blunt canines are hallmarks of this Hominin lineage.

Before the 1920's, knowledge of our fossilized ancestors only went back to our cousin species, the Homo Neanderthals or "the Neandarthal man" in Europe and some presumably earlier human-like forms from Java, in Southeast Asia. Only a handful of researchers were willing to estimate the time period of the earliest human ancestor at much more than 100,000 years, and there was no inkling of anything older from Africa. In addition, there was a predominant cognitive bias among the European paleoanthropologists against accepting early Africans as the ancestors of all humanity. However, despite all the obstacles put forward by personal unscientific biases, scientific investigation of the thinking society went on an eventually the search for our early ancestral species reached back in time far beyond 100,000 years ago. Slowly heaps of new empirical evidence began to emerge that eventually solidified the irrefutable fact of biological evolution that "we all come from Africa."

Today the oldest of all our hominin ancestors that we know of, is the *Sahelanthropus tchadensis* from Chad. This ancestral species of ours lived between 6 and 7 million years ago.

They had a combination of human-like and ape-like features. All our knowledge about this species is from nine cranial specimens discovered in Northern Chad by a research team of scientists led by French paleontologist Michael Brunet.

Figure 1.4 Reconstruction of S. tchadensis by sculptor Elisabeth Daynes

In the year 2001 Brunet and his team unearthed the first and so far the only fossil specimens of Sahelanthropus. This partial skull was named "Toumai" ("hope of life" in the local Daza language of Chad in central Africa). Before 2001, early humans in Africa had only been found in the Great Rift Valley in East Africa and sites in South Africa. Naturally the discovery of this early hominin species in West-Central Africa showed that the earliest hominins were more widely distributed than previously thought.

Despite the lack of post-cranial bones (bones below the skull), the cranial fossil materials tell us enough to know that Sahelanthropus had both ape-like and human-like features. Ape-like features included a small brain of around 360 cc (slightly smaller than a chimpanzee brain), sloping face, massive brow ridges (similar in thickness to male gorillas) and elongated skull. However, the position and orientation of the foramen magnum, that is the hole in the base of the skull through which the spinal cord passes, suggests that this ancestral species of ours stood and walked bipedally, with its spinal column held vertically as in modern humans rather than horizontally as in apes and other quadrupeds. Alongside the spinal cord opening underneath the skull, other prominent human-like features were small canine teeth and a short middle part of the face. They walked upright like humans which helped them survive in diverse habitats, including forests and grasslands.

After Sahelanthropus in the lineage of our hominin sub-family was *Orrorin tugenensis* which was discovered in the year 2001 from Eastern Africa. Orrorins were approximately the size of a chimpanzee and had small teeth with thick enamel, just like modern humans. In the Tugen Hills region of Central Kenya French paleontologist Brigitte Senut and French geologist Martin Pickford discovered more than a dozen early hominin fossils dating between about 6.2 million and 6.0 million years old.

Those fossils had previously unseen unique combination of ape-like and human-like characteristics for which they were given a new genus and species name, Orrorin tugenensis, which in the local language means "original man in the Tugen region". The upper femur of the species shows evidence of bone buildup that typically indicates one unique human-like quality - walking upright on two legs.

However, no skulls of Orrorin have been recovered, so its cranial morphology and brain size are uncertain. In both Orrorin and Sahelanthropus the canine teeth of males are larger and more pointed than in modern humans, but are small and blunt compared to the canines of male apes. Sahelanthropus tchadensis and Orrorin tugenensis are undeniably the oldest hominin species known so far. But there is a lot to be learnt about them and that is why they are not the best known early hominins. So far the best known early hominins are *Ardipithecus kadabba* and *Ardipithecus ramidus*. Their lifetime dates back to right after Sahelantropus and Orrorin.

Ardipithecus kadabba was discovered in the year 1997 from Eastern Africa. Paleoanthropologist Yohannes Haile-Selassie didn't at first realize that he had uncovered a new species when he discovered a piece of lower jaw in the Middle Awash region of Ethiopia. But the lower jaw specimen was followed by the discovery of 11 more specimens from at least 5 individuals, that paved the way for a new species. These specimens included hand, foot and toe bones, partial arm bones and a clavicle (collarbone). From the site of the fossil remnants faunal evidence was also found which implies that this early hominin ancestor of ours lived in a mixture of woodlands and grasslands. They had plenty of access to water via lakes and springs.

Originally those fossils were considered to be a subspecies of the previously discovered species Ardipithecus ramidus. It was not until 2004, that those specimens from Ethiopia were allocated to a new species. Six fossilized teeth discovered in 2002 at the site Aso Koma made it confirmed that the 1997 specimens were indeed unique. Thereafter in the year 2004 paleoanthropologists Yohannes Haile-Selassie, Gen Suwa and Tim White published an article allocating those fossils to a new species – Ardipithecus kadabba where "kadabba" means "oldest ancestor" in Afar language. As far as bodily characteristics are concerned, they walked upright and were similar in body and brain size to a modern chimpanzee. They existed between about 5.8 and 5.2 million years ago.

Thereafter existed another species of the genus Ardipithecus about 4.4 million years ago. It was Ardipithecus ramidus that was discovered before the discovery of the first kadabba fossil. In 1992–1993 a research team led by paleoanthropologist Tim White discovered the first Ardipitechus ramidus fossils that included seventeen fragments including skull, mandible, teeth and arm bones from the Afar region in the Middle Awash river valley of Ethiopia. More fragments were recovered in 1994, amounting to 45% of the total skeleton.

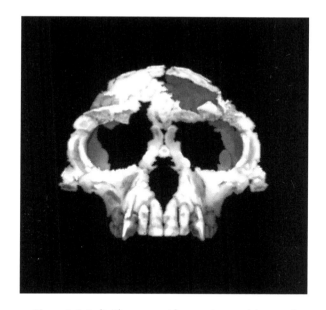

Figure 1.5 Ardipithecus ramidus specimen, nicknamed "Ardi"

At that time the most well established early human species were the Australopithecines. So, those fossils were originally described as a species of the genus Australopithecus, but White and his colleagues later in the year 2009 formally allocated them to a new genus, Ardipithecus as a new species Ardipithecus ramidus. In Afar language "Ardi" means "ground/floor" and "ramidus" means "root". However, the tern "pithecus" comes from the

Greek word "pithekos" which means "monkey". On October 1, 2009, paleontologists formally announced the discovery of the relatively complete A. ramidus fossil skeleton first unearthed in 1994. The fossil is the remains of a small-brained 50 kilogram (110 lbs.) female. And they nicknamed her as "Ardi".

Like most hominids, but unlike all previously recognized hominins, it had a grasping hallux or big toe adapted for locomotion in the trees. Like later hominins, they had reduced canine teeth. A. ramidus had a small brain, measuring between 300 and 350 cc which is slightly smaller than a modern bonobo or female chimpanzee brain, but much smaller than the brain of australopithecines like the famous Lucy (around 500 cc) and roughly 20% the size of the modern Homo sapiens brain. Some of Ardi's teeth are still connected to her jawbone and show enamel wear that clearly indicates a diet consisting of fruit and nuts. And last but not the least A. ramidus lived around 4.4 million years ago.

Now comes one of the most glorious discovery of the paleoanthropological society. It's the very much celebrated species of our beloved Lucy. A very important reason why Lucy is still so much celebrated is that she really embarrasses a lot of creationists. It makes us biologists rather pleased when creationists look up to Lucy as if she is not Lucy, but Lucifer the devil. Nevertheless, the creationists keep us naturalists in right track to some extent. They are the representation of primitive human stupidity at its extreme. And we need some stupidity in the society for true intellect to be adored.

This may jeopardize the pompous, theoretical and self-imposed vanity of the authoritarian, blood-sucking, modern-day fundamentalist hominins, but Adam and Eve are no more real than Clark Kent and Tony Stark, while Lucy and Ardi on the other hand, are as real as your grandparents. It is an incontrovertible evolutionary reality that Lucy and Ardi were indeed our distant grandmothers. Now let's get acquainted with our distant grandmother Lucy.

Her species is known as *Australopithecus afarensis*. They are one of the longest lived early hominin species. They lived between 3.85 and 2.95 million years. They lived for more than 900,000 years which is actually four times as long as our own species has been around. Lucy was discovered in 1974 near the village Hadar in Awash valley of the Afar region of Ethiopia by paleoanthropologist Donald Johanson. Lucy acquired her name from the Beatles' song "Lucy in the Sky with Diamonds", which was played loudly and repeatedly in the expedition camp all evening after the excavation team's first day of work.

In the year 2007, Lucy's fossils were assembled and exhibited publicly in a six-year tour of the United States. This exhibition was called Lucy's Legacy. It attracted remarkable public attention and made Lucy a household name around the globe.

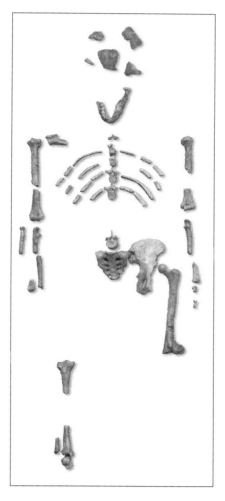

*Figure 1.6 Lucy - Australopithecus afarensis, cast from
Museum national d'histoire naturelle, Paris*

Figure 1.7 Au. afarensis reconstruction

Au. Afarensis had both ape-like and human-like characteristics. They had ape-like face proportion (a flat nose, a strongly projecting lower jaw) with a cranial capacity of around 500 cc and long, strong arms with curved fingers adapted for climbing trees. And as for human-like characteristics, they walked upright on two legs and had small canine teeth. The fossilized specimens imply that Lucy's species was adapted for living both in trees and on the ground. Such adaptation proved amazingly beneficial for their survival throughout almost a million years despite the climate shift.

After Lucy there existed another early human species in the Australopithecus genus, known as *Australopithecus africanus*. Their survival period was between 3.3 to 2.1 million years ago. The first fossils of Au. Africanus were found at the Taung site near Kimberley, South Africa in the year 1924. They were the fossil remnants that made us embark on a completely unique early hominin genus, which we know as Australopithecus. But for such a discovery, the road ahead is always long and filled with hardship. And in this case, the hardship was about 20 years long.

In 1924, workers at the Buxton Limeworks near Taung, South Africa, showed a fossilized primate skull to E. G. Izod, the visiting director of the Northern Lime Company. The director gave it to his son, Pat Izod, who put it on the mantle over his fireplace as a showpiece. When Josephine Salmons, a friend of the Izod family, paid a visit to Pat's home, she noticed the primate skull, identified it as from an extinct monkey and realized its possible significance to her mentor, Raymond Dart. Josephine Salmons was the first female student of Dart who was an anatomist at the University of Witwatersrand.

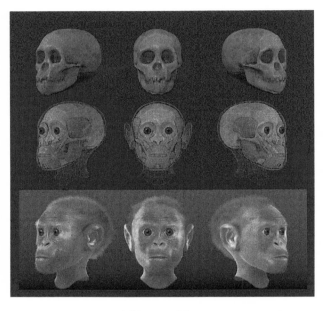

Figure 1.8 Taung child – Facial forensic reconstruction by Arc-Team

In the hands of Salmons that skull found its way to Dart. And naturally it stuck him as unique, so he asked the company to send any more interesting fossilized skulls should they be unearthed. He examined the skull and completed a paper that allocated the fossil as a new species of a new genus - Australopithecus africanus which means "southern ape from Africa". He described it as "an extinct race of apes intermediate between living anthropoids and man". His paper appeared in the 7 February 1925 issue of Nature. Also, that young Au. africanus skull was nicknamed the Taung Child.

Dart's theory was supported by Robert Broom. On April 18, 1947, Broom and John T. Robinson discovered a skull belonging to a middle-aged female with a brain capacity of 485 cc, while blasting at Sterkfontein about 40 kilometers northwest of Johannesburg. Broom classified it primarily as *Plesianthropus transvaalensis* (near-man from the Transvaal) and it was nicknamed Mrs. Ples. It was later classified as Au. africanus.

Au. africanus was anatomically a lot similar to Au. afarensis. It had a combination of human-like and ape-like features. Compared to Lucy's species, Au. africanus had a more round cranium housing and smaller teeth, but it also had some ape-like features including relatively long arms and a strongly sloping face that projects out from underneath the braincase with a prominent jaw. Like Au. afarensis, the pelvis, femur and foot bones of Au. africanus clearly imply that they walked bipedally, but the shoulder and hand bones indicate they were also adapted for climbing. The fossil remnants show that they eventually left the trees for life on the ground except when chased back sporadically by the big cats which dominated the area. Because of their massive jaws, they were believed to have had a diet similar to modern chimpanzees, that consisted of fruits, plants, fibrous roots, nuts, seeds, insects and eggs.

Even though no stone tools have been found in the sediments next to Au. africanus fossils, there are some indications in their fossils that they might have learnt to use stone tools. A 2015 study of hand bones in Au. africanus indicated that the species had "human-like trabecular bone pattern in the metacarpals consistent with forceful opposition of the thumb and fingers typically adopted during tool use," a pattern that would be consistent with an earlier adoption of tool manufacture and use than had been thought likely. However, we need further studies on this matter to be absolutely sure that Au. africanus did indeed learn to manufacture first stone tools. In terms of first stone tool manufacturing, Homo habilis is still officially hailed as the "handy man".

Other species of the genus Australopithecus were Au. anamensis, Au. garhi and Au. sediba. We also find some evidence that Au. garhi learnt to make primordial tools as well.

Australopithecines were believed to be scavengers who ate fibrous roots, tubers, seeds, and vegetation. They received more useable calories out of the starchy tubers and vegetable foods than did tree-dwelling chimpanzees. Natural selection favored the genes responsible for the enzyme amylase for "grounded" hominids because this savanna diet was much more readily available than the ape's diet in the trees. Occasionally, some of these early hominins may have hunted small prey and broke open bones left by other animals with small pebbles from riverbeds. But they were definitely not efficient hunters even of small animals. Mostly they were foragers who fed off the leftovers from lions and larger cats. They also used bones for digging their roots and fibers. Tool use was not that different from contemporary chimpanzees. Some have estimated their average life span to be 30 years but children and females were particularly vulnerable to the many larger carnivores. It was still not at all a safe environment. However, being upright meant that some of them could wield clubs for protection and carry food and other objects in their hands.

Eventually they left the forest altogether and moved to the savanna where their upright posture helped to see longer distances for scavenging food and watching for predators. Slowly their legs became longer and they developed arches in their feet allowing them to cover more ground than many of their four-legged cohabitants.

While living in the harsh environment of the wild, a very important tool of survival was being next to each other. This is what we call social organization. And our Australopithecine ancestors had a kind of basic social organization. The freaky surrounding compelled the Australopithecines to live in groups. Once they started to live in groups, they required further social skills in order to manage their social relationship, which in turn proved to be an important trigger for the increase in the brain size. By developing social skills the Australopithecines formed alliances and coalitions within the group in order to supervise their survival inside their society as well as outside of it.

With the limited cranial capacity of about 500 cc, the Australopithecines did indeed encounter the dawn of human consciousness. They were still very much primitive, at the same time they were primitively conscious. They developed a kind of emotional communication, which was confined to physical gestures and primitive vocalization. And such communication system had its own headache. Any negative emotional outbreak could disrupt harmony in the group. Such emotional outbreaks were followed by a lot of noises which attracted attention of the predators. Naturally, this created an adaptive pressure for cortical control of emotion and for the emergence of basic social emotions such as sympathy, guilt, and shame which promote cohesiveness. This triggered an increase in the brain size which was mostly in the neocortex that added an extra layer to the whole brain and made room for more neurons. In fact, their primitive form of social organization influenced the human brain to embark on an evolutionary journey of becoming the most social, emotional and advanced brain on planet earth.

There is one commonality among all of us humans, which is, we are all very much emotional. The foundation of this emotion part of the mind goes way back to the time of our early Australopithecine ancestors. The deep-rooted instinctual basis of emotions is to a great extent founded upon that early sociality of Lucy and other Australopithecines. We are very much indebted to those primordial ancestors of ours, for gifting us this amazing social and emotional brain.

The first hominin species that developed the first sophisticated stone tools was the Homo habilis. They lived between 2.4 and 1.4 million years ago. In 1994 they were given the name "handy man". However, now we have reason to think that older hominins like Au. garhi also developed primitive tools. Their tools may not have been as sophisticated as those of the habilis but they were sufficient to break bones and expose the marrow which could remain edible for a long time. This shift from a fruit enriched forest diet to a diet of scavenged meat set in motion a tripling of our ancestors' brains.

Sorry vegans! A vegetarian diet does indeed have health benefits, but if our ancestors had only lived on vegetables and had never touched meat, we would've never become the

eating meat enlarges brain size

smartest species on earth. And nor would the vegans have attained the moral sense of avoiding meat. Morally it may be better to not kill any creature for their flesh, but biologically, meat was one of the greatest factors involved in the rise of the psychology of thinking humanity. From an evolutionary standpoint, meat diet provided a great push towards the evolution of modern human consciousness.

The main biological hardware that generates this consciousness, that is the brain, increased significantly in size during the lifetime of one of the early hominin species of our own genus Homo, - the Homo habilis. During their lifetime of about 1 million years, their brain capacity increased tremendously from 550 cc to an astounding 800 cc. From a paleoanthropological perspective, Homo habilis was not that different physically from the Australopithecines and could be better seen as a late Australopithecine.

Between 1960 and 1963 at Olduvai Gorge in Tanzania a team of paleoanthropologists led by Louis and Mary Leakey unearthed the fossil remnants of a unique early human species. The first specimen was found by Jonathan Leakey, so it was nicknamed "Johny's Child". As those early fossil remnants had a unique combination of features different from the Australopithecines, Louis Leakey, South African Scientist Philip Tobias and British Scientist John Napier declared them a new species, "Homo habilis".

Similar to the Australopithecine ancestors, Homo habilis were scavengers and lived in social groups of around 70-80 individuals. For more social cohesion they required to develop further social intelligence. But they were still primitive and we still have found no indication of language capacity. So, communication was still limited to physical gestures, mimicry and primitive vocalization just like the Australopithecines.

Other than developing primitive stone tools, they didn't achieve any further technological or mental advancement. Like Au. garhi they survived on the dead animals' meat. They used their stone choppers to cut through the thick hides of dead animals and expose raw flesh. But the competition was huge. And those competitors were large and dangerous. Naturally, in order to win their meal, Homo habilis had to recruit new members in their group. This way the number of individuals in their groups eventually kept increasing.

With an increasing number of individuals in their groups, their social skills slowly became more and more advanced. Their intense social interaction proved to be the foundation of the development of language in the brain circuits.

Now the human ancestral lineage had reached the crossroads of evolution. Among all our primitive ancestors, now arrived the one that really was a primitive representation of modern advanced humans. They were the *Homo erectus*. They solved one of the most important pieces of human evolutionary puzzle. It was the mystery of fire.

Every animal on earth that had ever encountered fire, had run away from it. If Homo erectus could do the unimaginable and conquer their instinctive fear, they'd harness a new power. They just needed the nerve to reach into the blaze and they did. The impact of fire was an enormous step forward in human evolution.

Despite such an advancement of fire, due to the lack of ample brainpower and vocal structure, Homo erectus were still prelinguistic. However, their brain structure did go through some remarkable changes during the whole period of their existence. Their cranial capacity doubled from 550 to 1100 cc. With the addition of further neocortex layers, the frontal, temporal and parietal lobes increased in size. Cognitive functioning was more focused on imitation and mimicry involving vocalizations, facial expressions, eye movements and above all emotional expressions.

They might not have been so advanced in terms of intelligence, but they developed highly effective emotional communication. The brain of Homo erectus was also lateralized to create two different hemispheres. At an intellectual level, they developed more refined, symmetrical and sharper tools. They made advanced weapons and tools like hand axes, cleavers, and knives. This gave them the capacity to free themselves from the dictatorship of the harsh environment and survive in the harsher climates to which they traveled. They had already learnt to make and harness the natural gift of fire. This remarkable technological advancement along with refined tools gave Homo erectus heat, light and protection.

A Dutch surgeon named Eugene Dubois found the first fossilized Homo erectus in Indonesia in 1891. In 1894, Dubois named the species *Pithecanthropus erectus* that means "erect ape-man". At that time, Pithecanthropus (later changed to Homo) erectus was the most primitive of all known early human species. No early human fossils had been discovered in Africa yet. Homo erectus existed between 1.89 million and 143,000 years ago. It is possibly the longest lived early human species, about nine times as long as our own species has been around.

The most complete fossilized individual of this species is known as the "Turkana Boy". Microscopic study of the teeth indicates that he grew up at a growth rate similar to that of a great ape. There is fossil evidence that this species cared for old and weak individuals. The appearance of Homo erectus in the fossil record is often associated with the earliest hand axes, the first major innovation in stone tool technology.

They are the oldest known early humans to have possessed modern human-like body proportions with relatively elongated legs and shorter arms compared to the size of the torso. These features clearly indicate adaptations to a life lived on the ground. They lost the earlier tree-climbing adaptations and developed the ability to walk and possibly run long distances. Homo erectus is considered to have been the first species to have expanded beyond Africa. They migrated out of Africa to southern Asia and Europe about one million years ago. After developing advanced tools and learning to harness fire, they lived throughout the entire period of existence without any further advancement.

Over time, the body structure of our ancient ancestors became more robust with thicker bones and more muscle. And the perfect specimens for such robust body structure were the *Homo heidelbergensis* and *Homo neanderthalensis*. At a point of time both these species competed with Homo erectus. The existence of heidelbergensis dates back to between 700,000 and 200,000 years ago, while the Neanderthals lived between about 400,000 and 40,000 year ago.

Homo heidelbergensis were the first early hominin species to routinely hunt large animals. In the year 1908 near Heidelberg, Germany in the Rosch sandpit just north of the village Mauer, the first fossil specimen was discovered. German scientist Otto Schoentensack described the specimen as a completely new species.

Figure 1.9 Homo heidelbergensis, male. Reconstruction by John Gurche

This early ancestor of ours had a very large browridge, a larger braincase and a flatter face than all other previously known older hominins. Their robust body was the result of adaptation to colder climates. They took the torch of technological advancement one step further by building shelters for the first time in hominin history. As they migrated to colder climates, their bodies became more compact, which reduced overall skin surface area and heat loss. Such bodily adaption proved to be more efficient in conserving heat than a tall, lean body like Homo erectus, which exposed more surface area proportional to body mass useful in a hot, dry African environment.

Evidence reveals that H. heidelbergensis were the common ancestors of us Homo sapiens and our cousin species, the Neanderthals. Neanderthals diverged from H. heidelbergensis about 400,000 years ago in Europe and lived until about 40,000 years ago, while we the sapiens evolved about 200,000 years ago in Africa during a time of dramatic climate change.

As our cousins, Neanderthals are our closest extinct relatives. However, among the living relatives the closest are the chimpanzees. But the common ancestor of ours and the chimpanzees goes way back millions of years, while the common ancestor of ours and the Neanderthals existed as close as 200,000 years ago.

The Neanderthals had a larger headcase than us the sapiens. Their cranial capacity was an average of around 1500 cc, which is much larger than the average 1300 cc of modern humans. In the year 1829 the first specimens of fossilized Neanderthal skulls were discovered in Engis Caves, Belgium.

Then again in 1848 another skull was found in Forbes' Quarry, Gibraltar. But it was not until 1856, that those fossils were recognized as a new species. Johan Karl Fuhrott first recognized those fossils as "Neanderthal man", after the discovery of another similar kind of fossil in Neander valley near Mettmann, North Rhine-Westphalia, Germany. After this discovery, Geologist William King proposed the name "Homo neanderthalensis" at a meeting of the British Association for the Advancement of Science in 1864.

The tall, lean bodies of Homo erectus were adapted to tropical temperatures. Whereas the late hominin species Neanderthals were adapted to winter climates. Neanderthals were more heavily built than modern humans. With their huge cranial capacity of around 1500 cc they developed extraordinary taste in aesthetics. They occasionally made symbolic or ornamental objects. A very unique characteristic of Neanderthals was their primitive form of spirituality.

Figure 1.10 Reconstruction of the head of the Shanidar 1 fossil, a Neanderthal male who lived c. 70,000 years ago (John Gurche 2010)

Paleoanthropological evidence clearly shows that they deliberately buried their dead and even marked the graves with offerings, such as flowers. This implies that our cousin Neanderthals believed in some form of life after death. No other primates, and no earlier human species, had ever practiced this sophisticated and symbolic behavior. They may not have been so advanced as us, but among all the extinct hominin species Neanderthals were exceptionally advanced. They were amazingly rich in behavior. In terms of modern human consciousness, Homo neanderthalensis were right next to us.

Neanderthals were capable of symbolic thinking. Archeologists have unearthed shells containing pigment residues at two sites in the Murcia province of Southern Spain. Black sticks of the pigment manganese, which may have been used as body paint by Neanderthals, have previously been discovered in Africa. The pigment containers are the first significant evidence for their use of cosmetics. Until this discovery in the year 2010, it was thought that only the humans were conscious about their looks. But now it seems that Neanderthals really did engage in grooming their looks as well.

Their tools were unlike anything else made by other extinct hominins. These tools consisted of sophisticated stone-flakes, various hand axes and spears. They were even expert in building dugout boats, in which they navigated the Mediterranean Sea. They were pro hunters, who obtained most of their protein in their diet from animal sources. They knew how to create and control fire. They used caves for shelters as well as built beautiful homes using animal bones. And of course with their sophisticated tools they also made clothing. It has been speculated that Neanderthals had a proto-linguistic system of communication that was more musical than modern human language.

We the Homo sapiens existed side-by-side with Neanderthals for some time. The very first thing you must know about us is that the whole humanity emerged in Africa about 200,000 years ago. So, to anyone who knows the true history of humankind, "racism" is just an insignificant piece of social junk. According to genetic and anthropological evidence we evolved exclusively in Africa. So, we are all originally Africans. Over time as our ancestors began to spread throughout the world out from their homeland Africa, their physical characteristics started to show variations, simply by the natural force of adaptation. Thus, local population in one region of the earth, often appears different from those that live elsewhere. For example, northern Europeans often have blond hair, fair skin, and blue eyes, whereas those who have remained in Africa, or simply the Africans, have black hair, dark skin, and brown eyes.

These traits simply play a crucial role in the adaptation of particular populations to their environmental conditions. Blood groups may be associated with immunity to diseases more common in certain geographical areas, and dark skin shields the body from the damaging effects of ultraviolet radiation, which is much stronger in the tropical regions than in temperate regions. Humans are visually oriented, consequently, they have relied on visual cues - primarily skin color, to define races. However, when other types of characters, such as blood groups, are examined, patterns of variation correspond very poorly with visually determined racial classes.

In human beings, it is simply not possible to delimit clearly defined races that reflect biologically differentiated and well-defined groupings. Relatively little of the variation in the human species represents differences between the described races. Indeed, one study calculated that only 8% of all genetic variation among humans could be accounted for as differences that exist among racial groups. In other words, the human racial categories do a very poor job in describing the vast majority of genetic variation that exists in humans. For this reason, we the biologists reject the notion of human racial classifications as reflecting patterns of biological differentiation in the human species. And there is your scientific basis for dealing with each human being on his or her own merits and not as a member of a particular "race."

In short, the so-called human races do not reflect significant patterns of underlying biological differentiation. Biologically speaking, there is only race of humanity – that's human race. It is the same human heart that beats in every human being, regardless of the region. It is the same amount of zeal that runs through the veins of every human being, regardless of geological differences.

The only classification to be made out of humans should be based on character and nothing but the character. For example, from a common sociological standpoint, Tolstoy was a Caucasian, Gandhi was an Asian, and Martin Luther King Jr. was a Negro, yet all of their hearts were inspired by the one idea of nonviolent resistance. King received it from Gandhi, Gandhi received it from Tolstoy, and Tolstoy received it from Christ.

The same Sermon on the Mount that influenced Tolstoy to write "The Kingdom of God is Within You", inspired me to a great extent in my work "Principia Humanitas". In Principia Humanitas, to provide humanity a concrete mental foundation to manifest its innate humanism, I have said:

Am I a human? Or let me rephrase - am I a good human or a bad human? If the answer is in the affirmative side, which is in the side of goodness, then perhaps, you would deem me as a human being, in the truest sense of the term, but what if the answer is in the negative side – what if you figure out with your sense of moral compass, that I, Naskar is basically a bad human, a bad person, then what? Would I still be deemed by you and the society, as a real human being, or simply an imitation? That is the question. Are you a human or are you not? Forget nationality, forget race, forget color, forget religion. The real question that every member of the thinking humanity must ask – Am I a Human?

If the answer that appears in the mind is more in the track of nationality, ethnicity, religion, language, color or anything else, than in the track of being human, then the simple deduction is that one merely is an imitation of a glorious creature known as the human. That is the core principle of humanism – and in fact, that should be the core principle of thinking humanity. One can most gloriously hail oneself as a Christian, Jew, Muslim or a Hindu, or as American, Mexican, Asian, Russian, European or African, but the moment these self-imposed labels of heritage and culture take preference over the biological title of Human, it inadvertently destroys the very foundation of civilized human consciousness. So, in a world of civilized humans, one is first a human, then everything else.

Humanism is not a pompous philosophy to be talked and debated about by a handful of intellectuals - it is the purest form of moral compass, which defines the civilized heart of thinking humanity. It is not a luxury, rather an evolutionary necessity, if we are to keep evolving in the path of further mental and physical advancement, beyond the limitations imposed by the primitive ignorance of our wild past…

The point is, the Self is the measure of everything. And when one Self does genuine good to another Self, it is hailed as a real human being. Without this sense of oneness among humans, they don't deserve to be called as such. The edifice of conscience requires the pure backbone of one absolute Humanism, which never gets extinct with the cessation of a group of people like in a cult or religion, rather gets passed on from one human being to another so long as humanity thrives.

What then, are the basic principles of this quintessential core of real human existence? I depict, there are Five Core Principles of Humanism, that define real humans. Among these five, the first one is the Absolute Principle of Humanism.

First/Absolute Principle: *Self is All.*

Now, in an attempt to effectively define, illustrate and nourish this Absolute Principle of Humanism, or rather, to effectively nourish Humanism in the heart of the human society on the bed-rock of the Absolute Principle, four other principles come into action. I portray the four other principles of humanism, as follows:

Second: *Humans are the highest of beings in this world, above all mythical, mystical and godly figures. No God, Religion, Race or Nation is higher than the humans.*

Third: *The individual can attain a good life by harmoniously combining self-development with activities that contribute to the welfare of one's society.*

Fourth: *Basic assumptions, conjectures, convictions, fantasies and mysticism that are thrown towards the mind, must go through rigorous analysis and questioning by the individual, before being either accepted or rejected.*

Fifth: *One life is all we have, and as such, one should make the most out of it. Death is the ultimate cessation of the individual Self.*

These Five Principles of Humanism, are to be the cornerstones of the conscientious global society of real humans. On the outside these may seem as five different principles, but when you delve deep into them, all you discover is the Absolute Oneness of all Humans. Humanity should be defined by one Humanism, not by the superficial, prejudicial and pompous citadels of differentiation.

The human heart is first a human heart, then everything else - American, Christian, Asian, Jew, or whatever. There is only label worth fighting for, nay, not fighting for, that is "human". A human heart should be measured by the ideas, values and sentiments it nourishes within, and nothing else. Remember, a heart, without an idea to live for – without a principle to live by – without a sentiment to live on, is simply a lifeless object, an empty cup, yet to serve its purpose. And once a glorious idea, a vivacious principle and a radiant sentiment, are poured into the heart, it becomes a beacon of hope for all humanity. And this beacon, my friend, has no race – it has no color – it has no ethnicity – all that it has is the power to pass on courage, conscience and goodwill to the coming generations.

Ideas that drive humanity know no bounds of racial discrimination. Sentiments that glorify humanity know no racial distinction. A mother's love for her child is the same anywhere in the world. A man's concern for his family is the same anywhere in the world. A sister's care for her brother is the same anywhere in the world. Every single characteristic that defines a true human being is the same anywhere in the world.

CHAPTER II
Neurobiology of Racism

In the biological sense, race does not exist. However, it does exist quite distinctively in the sociological perspective. In fact, race is a sociological construct formed out of the primordial need to distinguish one's own hereditary identity from that of others'. Nevertheless, such varied cultural nuances in human population, is more reason to celebrate each other's diversities than to make walls of differentiation out of them. These variations are no civilized basis for discrimination. if anything, they are what make our species the most unique one.

To make a certain dish you need various ingredients. Take one ingredient away and the dish would be incomplete. Such is the case of the humankind. It is a magnificent cuisine made of ethnicities and cultural variations. Take any one of these variations away, and humanity would lose its soul, for these variations collectively construct the glorious soul of our species.

Racial discrimination is a primordial feature of the human mind, quite similar to promiscuity - it is not a quality of the civilized conscience. To put in simple terms, good and evil are both fundamental features of the human mind – it is through millions of years of cerebral evolution, that the good and civilized portion of the mind became strong enough to have a firm grip over the much older evil and primitive portion. Racism is an extreme form of cognitive bias which wreaks havoc in the society, when unchecked by the conscience.

Every single human being is neurologically predisposed to be biased in various walks of life. It is biologically impossible to be absolutely free from all biases, nevertheless, the more a person rigorously trains the self to be rational and conscientious, the more that self becomes strong enough to keep the biases in check, never to let them run rampant over the psyche.

The human brain always concocts biases to aid in the construction of a coherent mental life, exclusively suitable for an individual's personal needs. Some of these biases are fundamentally positive, or at the very least, not sociologically destructive, such as a man thinking his wife to be the most beautiful woman on earth, while some others are straight-away negative and quite catastrophic, such as an American thinking all Mexican and Muslim immigrants are drug-dealers or terrorists, simply because of their ethnicity or religion. One way or another we are all biased, but still we have the modern cortical capacity to choose whether or not to let the harmful biases dictate our behavior – we can choose whether or not to let them hijack our moral compass – we can choose whether or not to let them turn us into empty shells with no trace of character inside. Hence, the real battle is within yourself.

Now let's conduct a biopsy of racial bias and attempt to recognize its biological origin in the brain. For this, first we need to have a basic understanding of the human brain. In this twenty-first century most people have a rough idea of what the brain looks like. It has two mirror-image halves, called the cerebral hemispheres, and resembles a walnut sitting on top of a stalk, called brainstem. Each hemisphere is divided into four lobes: the frontal lobe, the parietal lobe, the occipital lobe, and the temporal lobe.

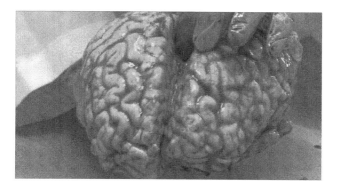

Figure 2.1 Two Hemispheres of the Brain

The occipital lobe at the back of your head is concerned with vision. Damage to this region can result in blindness. The temporal lobe is responsible for mostly hearing, and certain aspects of visual perceptions, along with the unique human feature of religious sentiments. Anomalous activity in the neural network of this region, often leads to experiences that people tend to define as religious or spiritual.

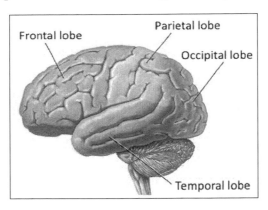

Figure 2.2 Four Lobes of the Brain

The parietal lobe is concerned with constructing your perception of the external world. It simulates a three dimensional representation of the spatial layout of the environment you live in, and also of your own body within that three dimensional representation. And lastly the frontal lobes, are perhaps the most enigmatic of all the brain regions. They are concerned with some very exuberant aspects of the human mind, such as your moral sense, your wisdom, your ambition and other mysterious activities of the mind, which we have only started to understand.

The cerebral hemispheres contain higher nerve centers responsible for various sensory and motor information. Whereas the brain stem contains neural networks that constitute lower nerve centers for the control of vital functions of the body such as breathing, blood pressure regulation, sleeping, eating, heart rate monitoring etc. To put it simply, the brain stem modulates vital processes of your body, without your conscious awareness of involvement. Because, consciousness itself is the functional expression of mostly the higher nerve centers residing in the cerebral hemispheres.

The brain stem is divided into three distinct parts: medulla oblongata, pons and midbrain.

The midbrain contains groups of neurons that project up to the cerebral hemispheres. These neurons modulate bodily functions like alertness, temperature regulation, pleasure etc.

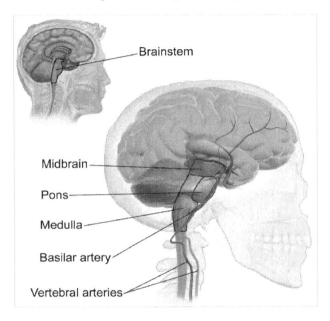

Figure 2.3 The Brain Stem consists of three parts – the midbrain, medulla, and pons

The pons lies between the medulla oblongata and the midbrain. It contains tracts that carry signals from the cerebral hemispheres to the medulla and to the cerebellum and also tracts that carry sensory signals to the thalamus.

Cerebellum is a beautiful neuronal machine of the brain whose intricate cellular architecture plays an absolutely central role in the control and timing of movements. It receives input from sensory systems of the spinal cord and from other parts of the brain, and integrates these inputs to fine-tune motor activity or muscle movement. Damage to this little part of the brain leads to poorly coordinated movements, loss of balance, slurred speech, cognitive difficulties and also motor learning disability. The cerebellum is vital for motor learning and adaptation.

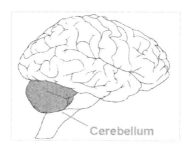

Figure 2.4 Cerebellum provides you with smooth, coordinated body movement

Almost all of your voluntary actions rely on fine control of motor circuits, and the cerebellum is important in their optimal adjustment, with respect to timing. It has a very regular cortical arrangement and seems to have evolved to bring together vast amounts of information from the sensory systems, the cortical motor areas, the spinal cord and the brainstem.

Imagine yourself playing catch. If you are a pro player, then it apparently seems so easy to catch the ball coming towards you. But underneath that simple action of catching the ball, lies intricate neural functioning of the cerebellum. It carries out countless electrochemical tasks inside its architecture with the help of higher nerve centers of the brain, to enable you to perceive the whole situation - the position of the ball, its speed, its distance from you, the projectile of its motion. And the end product of such fine tuning of neural functioning, is you catching the ball with a blink of an eye.

Now before we move on to the brain structures containing higher nerve centers, let me give you a brief introduction to the third part of the brainstem. While talking about the midbrain and pons, we shifted our attention a little towards the brain region called cerebellum, the very neural architecture that is fine tuning your body posture right at this very moment, while you are reading this book. It is making sure that you are comfortable enough to pay attention to the pages, that are explaining to you its very functioning.

Now, the third part of the brainstem is known as medulla oblongata, or just medulla. It is the lower half of the brainstem continuous with the spinal cord. Its upper part is continuous with the pons. Right in front of the cerebellum, the medulla is cone-shaped neural mass that connects the higher levels of the brain to the spinal cord.

It is responsible for several functions of the autonomous nervous system:

1. Respiration – Medulla modulates respiration process with the use of chemoreceptors that transduce a chemical signal into an action potential. These receptors detect changes in acidity of the blood, thus if the blood is considered too

acidic by the medulla, electrical signals are sent to intercostal muscles of the chest cavity, increasing their contraction rate in order to reoxygenate the blood,

2. Cardiac functioning – Heart rate monitoring.

3. Vasomotor functioning – Regulation of blood pressure with the use of baroreceptors, that sense blood pressure,

4. Modulating reflex actions of vomiting, coughing, sneezing, and swallowing. These reflexes which include the pharyngeal reflex, the swallowing reflex (also known as the palatal reflex), and the masseter reflex, can be termed, bulbar reflexes.

In short medulla oblongata plays a crucial role in maintaining homeostasis in your body.

Now let's go deeper into the brain to discover the structures that together construct all the emotional features of our mental life.

Right above the brainstem, there is a system of inexplicable properties. It is the very heart of all your emotions. It is the complex neural architecture, that combines higher mental functions and emotional responses into one system. I am talking about a fascinating part of the brain, known as the Limbic System. Let me give you a little example to show the significance of this system in human life.

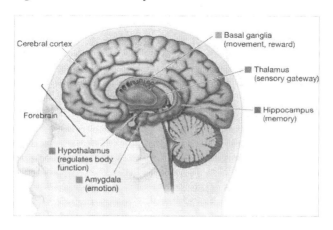

Figure 2.5 The Limbic System surrounded by the layers of Cerebral Cortex

When you say to someone "follow your heart", it actually refers to the rhetorical representation of various emotions, that are precisely produced from neural activity of the limbic system. So, the metaphoric heart we always boast about while giving advice to our friends, is actually not anywhere near the biological organ known as heart. Rather it too, like all other elements of the human mind exists only in the brain. This is why we often refer to the limbic system as the emotional nervous system.

The Limbic System is a complex set of structures found just beneath the cerebrum. It is not only responsible for our rich and colorful emotional lives, but also some of our higher mental functions, such as learning and formation of memories. The limbic system is composed of several structures, each of which plays crucial role in simulating our mental lives. They are the amygdala, hippocampus, thalamus, hypothalamus, fornix, parahippocampal gyrus and cingulate gyrus.

Now let's have a basic idea of how various structures of the limbic system take part in our mental activities.

In the limbic system, an almond shaped structure located deep within the brain called the amygdala is the mind's emotion-coordinating system. From the amygdala emotional impulses go to the hypothalamus (the brain's Homeostasis center). Then the hypothalamus raises the blood pressure, heart rate and breathing, and puts the body into fight-or-flight mode based on the intensity of the emotional impulses. The amygdala also alerts the cerebral cortex (the brain's Intelligence center) which analyses the emotional situation and decides how much attention is required in that specific scenario. If the intensity of the emotional impulses is high enough then the higher nerve centers of the conscious brain become alert and strong conscious emotional sensation kicks in. Then the prefrontal cortex (the brain's decision-making center) in the frontal lobes plays its part by determining how to respond to the situation.

From an evolutionary perspective, one of the most fundamental role of the amygdala is to identify danger and trigger a sense of fear and alertness in the face of that danger. Such primitive fear response of the amygdala is necessary for self-preservation. Hence, the element of fear in our mental lives, is not actually an enemy. Rather, fear is wisdom in the face of danger, that we have acquired through millions of years of struggle in the wild.

Amygdala's neural connections to the rest of the brain put it in a unique position to rapidly respond to sensory input and influence physiological and behavioral responses, as well as to influence memory formation in the adjacent hippocampus, the memory indexer.

One of the most common characteristics of our limbic system is that, the stronger our amygdala responds to a situation filled with emotional potential, the more details of that situation is indexed by the hippocampus. The hippocampus is the brain's memory formation center, which is found deep within the brain, shaped like a sea horse. It consists of two horns that curve back from the amygdala. This little seahorse of your brain connects minute emotional senses like smell, sound or taste to memories and send the memories out to the appropriate part of the cerebral hemisphere for long-term storage.

Now comes the Thalamus. This little structure is endowed with one of the most significant features of your mental life. And it literally plays the most significant role when we talk about the human consciousness. Note that, I said, it plays the most significant role in consciousness, not one of the most. What could be so significant, one might wonder?

The thalamus literally modulates your very consciousness, by regulating the mental states of sleep and wakefulness. It plays a major role in regulating the level of your conscious awareness. Hence, damage to the thalamus can lead a person permanently to coma. It is also involved in relaying sensory and motor information to the cerebral cortex.

Right below the thalamus, resides the hypothalamus, which is the brain's Homeostasis center. It is responsible for various autonomic functions of the body, such as regulating body temperature, hunger, thirst, fatigue etc. It also controls daily cycles (circadian rhythms) in physiological states and behaviors such as sexual behavior. Another important function of the hypothalamus is to link the nervous system with the endocrine system via the pituitary gland.

The hypothalamus has a central role in neuroendocrine system of the body, most notably by its control of the anterior pituitary, which in turn regulates various endocrine glands and organs. Thus, it coordinates the rhythmic release of eight major hormones in the body.

Ultimately the profound regulatory influences of Hypothalamus over physiological and behavioral processes act as an essential feature in the path of survival.

Other few structures of the limbic system have their own responsibilities. The Fornix is involved in recalling a specific memory. Parahippocampal Gyrus is involved in memory formation and recalling visual scene. The Cingulate Gyrus participates in emotional anticipation. It also coordinates smells and sights, with pleasant memories of previously experienced emotions.

The sensory neurons of your entire nervous system that is spread throughout the body, receive crucial data from the external world, and based on that information, the neural circuits of various structures in the brain, construct all the elements of your mental lives. And these magnificent elements, such as emotions, ambitions, dreams, awareness, divinity, behaviors, personality etc. are collectively known as the human mind.

These elements also include our racial attitudes and behaviors. It is the interactive activation of a few distinct brain structures that gives rise to the unintentional, implicit expression of racial attitudes and its control. Over the past few decades, we scientists interested in the mental representation of race and ethnicity have increasingly turned to electrophysiology, functional magnetic resonance imaging (fMRI) and other physiological methods to address how individuals process, evaluate and utilize human variation along the social dimension of race in decision-making in everyday interactions. These new tools push the frontiers of our understanding of how humans perceive and evaluate race and how these processes relate to the type of social behaviors that have consequential effects for the perceiver and the perceived. They yield insights into how to address the unintended expressions of racial attitudes, including those that diverge from conscious attitudes.

The portion of the brain that we have found most intriguing in our studies of racial attitude and its control, is a network of regions that includes the amygdala, anterior cingulate cortex (ACC), dorsolateral prefrontal cortex (DLPFC) and fusiform face area (FFA). Here the amygdala and the DLPFC are the most important regions, the former being the main brain structure responsible for eliciting an aversive emotional response to racial or ethnic differences, and the later being the brain structure of the civilized mind that tames that response. Now, let's delve deep into each of these structures and their functions to understand their contribution to what we today call Racism or Ethnic Discrimination.

The amygdala, a subcortical structure in the anterior temporal lobe, is the brain area that has been most reported with greatest frequency in studies of black-white race attitudes, beliefs and social decision-making. It comprises a small group of nuclei that are critical for the acquisition, storage and expression of classical fear conditioning. The amygdaloid fear response is an evolutionary wisdom which plays a crucial role in learning. Fear, in one form or another, teaches a person to stay alert for any ensuing existential crisis.

In our modern neuroscientific community, amygdala is an exceptionally intriguing region of the limbic system, but it did not stand out as an important brain structure until 1956 when Weiskrantz showed that the emotional components of a pathological condition named Kluver-Bucy syndrome, which is a symposium of behavioral consequences of temporal lobe damage, such as hyperphagia and hypersexuality, were due to the involvement of the amygdala.

In the 30's of the 20th century, two scientists - Heinrich Kluver and Paul Bucy - described the role of temporal lobe in regulation of emotional states. They did bilateral temporal lobectomies (which also involved the amygdales, situated deep within the lobes) in Rhesus monkeys. The procedure resulted in a dramatic change in their behavior, described by Kluver himself as the most striking and apparent alteration ever observed in consequence of surgical experiments performed on animal brains. Kluver and Bucy divided the symptoms into six major groups:

1. "Mental blindness", today referred to as visual agnosia – inability to visually recognize objects in spite of normal visual acuity,

2. Hypermetamorphosis – the urge to react to every visual stimulus,

3. Change of dietary habits, e.g. eating large amounts of meat (the type of behavior was rarely observed in monkeys),

4. "Oral tendency" – the so-called oral perception – examination of objects by mouth through licking, sucking and chewing,

5. Emotional changes (one of the most distinct symptoms) – complete obliteration of fear responses to threatening painful stimuli, docility and loss of the so-called defensive aggression, diminished emotional reactivity (at times even completely obliterated, particularly apparent in case of aversive and painful stimuli), loss of social behaviors,

6. Changes in sexual behaviors, increased sex drive, hetero and homosexual behaviors, autosexuality.

Shortly after the discovery of Kluver and Bucy, similar neurobehavioral disturbances were observed also in humans following bilateral temporal lobe damage. The cluster of symptoms was then named as Kluver-Bucy syndrome (KBS). The first description of a patient with the syndrome originates from 1955 - this was a patient after bilateral temporal lobectomy due to drug-resistant epilepsy. In humans, KBS syndrome is a constellation of the following symptoms:

reversal of emotional states (loss of fear and defense responses to pain or general disinhibition combined with euphoria), hypermetamorphosis, hyperorality (hypherphagia, bulimia, the so called "raging hunger"), sex drive disturbances (leading towards masturbation).

Kluver-Bucy syndrome thus attracted the attention of the medical community towards the brain's fear response circuits - a lot had to be learnt. For this, scientists turned towards the experiment of classical conditioning (originally known as "conditional reflex") by the Russian physiologist Ivan Petrovich Pavlov (1849-1936). He discovered the concept of conditional reflex while examining the rates of salivations among dogs. Pavlov was fascinated to notice that when a bell (conditioned stimulus) was rang followed by presentation of food (unconditioned stimulus) to a dog in consecutive sequences, it would initially salivate when the food was presented. But eventually, the dog would come to associate the sound with the presentation of the food and salivate immediately upon the presentation of that conditioned stimulus of sound, even without the presentation of the unconditioned stimulus of food.

Pavlov's assistant Ivan Filippovitch Tolochinov who was with him the whole time during the experiment, presented the results at the Congress of Natural Science in Helsinki in the year 1903. Late the same year, at the 14th International Medical Congress in Madrid, Pavlov himself explained his findings in detail by reading his paper entitled "The Experimental Psychology and Psychopathology of Animals." His experiment earned him the Nobel Prize in Physiology/Medicine in the year 1904.

Further through the writings of John B. Watson and B. F Skinner, Pavlov's idea of conditioning as an automatic form of learning became a key concept in the then developing field of comparative psychology.

To have a basic idea of the brain's fear response circuits, Pavlov's concept of classical conditioning is exactly what we needed. In our experiments we called it *Pavlovian Fear Conditioning*.

In the late 1970s and early 80s, researchers began using a simple behavioral task of Pavlovian fear conditioning, to study fear circuits. This was a huge leap forward in the path of understanding the brain's fear response.

In Pavlovian fear conditioning, an emotionally neutral conditioned stimulus (CS), usually a tone, is presented to rodents in combination with an aversive unconditioned stimulus (US), often a footshock. As a result of such pairing, eventually the rodents form an associative memory between the CS and US.

After training of several such pairings, the conditioned stimulus acquires the capacity to elicit responses that typically occur in the presence of danger (as the unconditioned stimulus of footshock feels like danger to the rodents), such as defensive behavior (freeze or flee responses), autonomic nervous system responses (changes in blood pressure and heart rate), neuroendocrine responses (release of hormones from the pituitary and adrenal glands) etc.

These responses are neither learned nor voluntary. They are innate, evolutionarily typical responses to any kind of threat and are expressed automatically in the presence of appropriate stimulus.

Thus, fear conditioning allows new or learned threats to automatically activate very basic evolutionarily tuned instinctual responses to danger. Such fear conditioning happens in nature to all species all the time, including humans. It enables a species to learn about new threats. And our rodent model provides a valuable way to understand the neurobiology and behavioral psychology of this instinctual fear response.

Amygdaloid Fear Conditioning or simply Fear Conditioning depends on the convergence of conditioned stimulus and unconditioned stimulus information in the amygdala. The CS-

US association occurs in the amygdala via an intriguing synaptic process called *Long-Term Potentiation*, where the existing synaptic connections are strengthened through the release of more neurotransmitter in the synaptic cleft based on their recent activity.

Let's have a little more insight of this amazing synaptic strengthening mechanism. At the end of the 19th century, researchers recognized that the number of neurons in the adult brain – a hundred billion – did not increase with age. This fantastic revelation gave the neuroscientists good enough reason to believe that formation of new memories was not the result of the genesis of new neurons. With this realization came the need to explain, how else could new memories be formed if not through the formation of new neurons?

The father of Neuroscience, Santiago Ramón y Cajal proposed the idea that memories might be formed by strengthening the connections between existing neurons in the pursuit of improving the efficacy of their communication.

Cajal's idea echoed further in the celebrated theory of Hebbian Learning introduced by Donald Hebb, in his 1949 book The Organization of Behavior. Donald Olding Hebb (1904-1985) was a Canadian psychologist who made a crucial contribution in the neuropsychology of learning. In fact, he is often hailed as the father of neuropsychology.

"The Organization of Behavior" is considered to be Hebb's most significant contribution to the field of neuropsychology. As a combination of his years of work in brain surgery mixed with his study of human behavior, it finally brought together the two realms of human perception that for a long time could not be linked properly together.

Donald O. Hebb's The Organization of Behavior connected the fascinating domain of Neuroscience with the mysterious realm of Psychology.

In this book, he introduced the Hebbian theory, as a plausible explanation for the adaptation of neurons in the brain during learning process. It describes a basic mechanism for synaptic plasticity, where an increase in synaptic efficacy arises from the presynaptic neuron's repeated and persistent stimulation of the postsynaptic neuron.

In the book Hebb states:

"Let us assume then that the persistence or repetition of a reverberatory activity (or "trace") tends to induce lasting cellular changes that add to its stability. The assumption can be precisely stated as follows: When an axon of cell A is near enough to excite a cell B and, repeatedly or persistently takes part in firing it, some growth process or metabolic change takes place in one or both cells such that .A's efficiency, as one of the cells firing B, is increased."

Through various experiments and studies, Hebbian theory of learning through synaptic strengthening has been well established as an irrefutable fact of Neuroscience. But such a theory was farsighted for Hebb's time. In the late 19th and early 20th century neuroscientists and psychologists were not equipped with the neurophysiological techniques necessary for elucidating the biological underpinnings of learning in animals. These skills would not come until the later half of the 20th century, at about the same time as the discovery of long-term potentiation.

Long-Term Potentiation (LTP) was first discovered by the neurophysiologist Terje Lomo, through a series of neurophysiological experiments on anesthetized rabbits to explore the role of the hippocampus in short-term memory. In a 2003 paper, Lomo writes:

"In 1966, I had just begun independent work for the degree of Dr medicinae (PhD) in Per Andersen's laboratory in Oslo after an eighteen-month apprenticeship with him. Studying the effects of activating the perforant path to dentate granule cells in the hippocampus of anaesthetized rabbits, I observed that brief trains of stimuli resulted

in increased efficiency of transmission at the perforant path-granule cell synapses that could last for hours. In 1968, Tim Bliss came to Per Andersen's laboratory to learn about the hippocampus and field potential recording for studies of possible memory mechanisms. The two of us then followed up my preliminary results from 1966 and did the experiments that resulted in a paper that is now properly considered to be the basic reference for the discovery of LTP."

After its original discovery in the rabbit hippocampus, neuroscientists have observed LTP in a variety of other neural structures, including cerebral cortex, cerebellum, amygdala and some others. Based upon all the neuroscientific evidence, we can say that it is very much plausible that LTP occurs in mammalian brains as well, including us humans. In the next chapter I shall further elaborate the cellular mechanism of LTP in detail.

Through this very process of Long-Term Potentiation the association of conditioned stimulus and unconditioned stimulus occurs in the amygdala, that in turns enables a species to learn about new threats, it encounters in the environment. It all happens through the strengthening of synaptic connections of neurons in the basolateral complex of the amygdala. And the end product of such synaptic strengthening is a primitive instinctual fear response to an apparently new perceived threat. Thus, the brain simply reacts to the modern threats of the human society, in a way it used to react during its primordial day of survival in the wild.

Production of the fear response to any kind of unpleasant stimulus (conditioned or unconditioned), depends on the central nucleus of the amygdala, which coordinates the output of defensive responses through downstream connections with response-specific brain centers. For example, fear responses like freezing and conditioned analgesia (suppression of pain upon exposure to an aversive stimulus) are modulated by the brain region called "periaqueductal gray", located around the cerebral aqueduct within the tegmentum of the midbrain. While on the other hand, another kind of fear response, like potentiated startle is mediated by the brain center called "reticularis pontis caudalis" or "caudal pontine reticular nucleus".

In the fear responses of the amygdala, hippocampus plays a crucial role as well. Over time the hippocampus forms memories of the entire context of the unpleasant stimulus (in case of animals, the chamber in which the pair of CS and US were presented, becomes the context, and as a result of this contextual fear, they exhibit fear responses when returned to the chamber). And proper functioning of the hippocampus is necessary for a new aversive stimulus to condition a creature for a fear response. For example, in case of amnesia in humans, lesions of the hippocampus made shortly after conditioning produce a severe and selective deficit of contextual fear, whereas those made a month or more after training have little or no effect on contextual fear. This happens because, the hippocampus is the brain's memory indexer that transforms short term memory into long term, by sending the newly attained memories out to various regions of the cerebral cortex for long-term storage. This conversion process is called memory consolidation. And once the memory of a context is consolidated, it becomes independent of the hippocampus.

- *What is Mind?*

Thus, the amygdala with the help of other limbic system structures contributes immensely to the survival of a species. It is done through the association of a certain stimulus with emotions. And it is the amygdala's role in the detection of emotional relevance of a certain stimulus that inspired the first investigations of its contributions to racial attitudes of the human society. The history of race relations in various corners of the world, is fraught with complex irrational emotional responses of the amygdala, including fear, hostility and lack of trust, triggered by distinct ethnic stimuli. Consistent with the emotional salience of race in various cultures throughout the world, numerous studies have revealed greater amygdaloid activity in response to outgroup race face, that is, faces judged as belonging to a race group different from oneself, than to ingroup faces.

It is just like the male evolutionary libidinal response evoked by the visual stimulus coming from the sight of a beautiful lady even when that man is quite happily married. It is the top-down executive control of the prefrontal cortex that does not let such primitive emotional response manifest through behavior. It is because of this prefrontal executive control that not every married man is off to cheat on his wife with every other beautiful colleague who comes along his way. It is because of this truly human faculty that not every American is out on the streets shouting – "when Mexico sends its people, they are sending drug-dealers and rapists." It is because of the healthy functioning of this cognitive faculty that not every famous personality is found saying - "when you are a star, they let you do anything, even grab women by their vagina".

In this context, a specific portion of the prefrontal cortex, known as the Dorso-Lateral Prefrontal Cortex (DLPFC) is an extremely crucial brain region to be acquainted with. It is the part of the PFC that is highly involved in the cognitive regulation of emotion, by modulating responses in the amygdala and striatum through its connectivity with the ventro-medial prefrontal cortex. Another brain region called the anterior cingulate cortex (ACC) is involved in performance monitoring, whereas the DLPFC is involved in implementing the control. Dysregulation in either region can lead to reductions in self-control, either through a failure to note a potential error or a failure to implement task- or goal-appropriate responses. Studies of race processing reveal that the DLPFC works in concert with the ACC. While the ACC works on detecting a conflict between conscious intentions and implicit attitudes, the DLPFC works on engaging a regulatory mechanism to control unwanted, implicit racial associations.

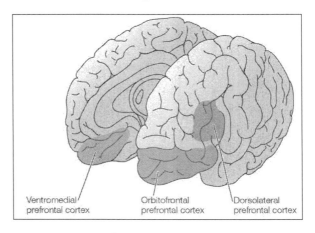

Figure 2.6 Prefrontal Cortex Regions involved in decision-making

ACC is involved in monitoring for response competition and, once a conflict is detected, serves to engage executive control. In the race context, conflict between automatic, implicit feelings and conscious intentions to respond fairly may explain the involvement of the ACC. Equality norms in, say American society, dictate that behaving in a racially biased manner is unacceptable, and many individual Americans share that civilized aspiration. Ironically, although contemporary cultural norms stress equality and fairness, the Western culture is also saturated with negative associations of the black population. Thus, for many individuals, conflict persists at a neurological level between civilized, conscientious, egalitarian goals and automatic negative attitudes and stereotypes.

A number of studies report evidence of ACC activation in response to black and white faces, and a few suggest that BOLD response patterns reflect conflict between implicit, automatic race attitudes and explicit, intentional race beliefs about equality. In simple terms, this means that, ACC is the most significant organ in terms of reflecting the internal battle between the civilized conscience and primitive instincts of an individual mind. The Anterior Cingulate Cortex is the distinctive brain region where the real battle between good and evil is seen most vividly. Another brain region that is involved in this battle is the Fusiform Face Area, as it is responsible for facial recognition.

Alongside the activation of the ACC, as the DLPFC boldly engages itself in resolving the conflict, slowly it takes control of the situation and eventually the civilized conscience of the thinking individual emerges triumphant. This battle between good and evil can more vibrantly be demonstrated with the case of male sexuality. Due to obvious evolutionary reason, men are more primordial in the domain of sexual pursuit than women. For a man, the optimal evolutionary strategy is to disseminate his genes as widely as possible, given his few minutes or, alas, seconds, of investment in each encounter. While on the contrary, a woman invests a great deal of time and effort - a nine months long, risky, laborious pregnancy, in each offspring.

Naturally, over the course of millions of years, women have evolved into a more monogamous creature than men, when in a relationship, while on the other hand, the tendency of men is to be promiscuous. Now the question that may rise in your mind is, if men are biologically more polygamous and

WE ARE ALL BLACK

women are more monogamous, then how can a romantic relationship ever last for long?

The answer lies in the executive control of the prefrontal cortex. It is true that men will always be men with their innate wild attraction towards large breasts and big even while being in a relationship. But through the process of Natural Selection, the amazing brain region called the prefrontal cortex evolved inside the skull, to keep that beast under control.

This little portion of the cerebral cortex endows the mind with the ability to keep all your momentary and quite irrational and uncivilized emotional impulses in check. The entire cerebral cortex is the crowning achievement of primate evolution. It is the constructor of all your inexplicably modern and typically human faculties. It is the part of the brain that most distinctively sets us apart from any other species on this planet.

By putting selective pressure over the hominin brain, Mother Nature made the human brain circuits go through not only quantitative but also qualitative changes, over the period of a few million years. And these changes are most significant in the Cerebral Cortex. In fact, the principles governing the cortical development hold the key to understanding our cognitive capacity of intelligence, creativity and conscience.

You must remember, that all your pride of being superior to all other animals on earth, is predicated on the functions of the Cerebral Cortex. Without the highly advanced and complicated neural processes of the cortex, there is no difference between us and other animals.

The human cerebral cortex is a laminated structure composed of the most bewildering diversity of neurons arranged in distinct patterns among all the species on earth. We are what we are because of this diversity of neurons in the cerebral cortex. This diversity enables us to become the most advanced as well as civilized species on this planet. However, the human mind also has a neurological predisposition to act in profoundly wild and uncivilized ways, thus producing inhuman behavioral expressions such as Racism. All of these primitive responses emerge from the innate biological predisposition of monstrosity, which lies within the deepest region of the human brain – the limbic system, right below the layers of the cerebral cortex.

Most of the limbic brain, including the amygdala that is responsible for eliciting primitive racist attitudes, has been there since our reptilian days. The face of this ancient region of the brain is shameless and ill-mannered. It is a wild beast that does not play well with any kind of social norms, unlike the civilized face of the cerebral cortex. These two faces of your mind are completely opposite of each other, yet they work together to keep you up on your feet. It is the fascinating interplay between the Cerebral Cortex and Limbic System, that makes our species a wonderful and unique blend of emotions and values.

Like all other mental and physical faculties of the human species, the cortical executive control over emotions evolved out of a growing need to survive in the dreadful environment of the wilderness. Like I said in the previous chapter, it began with our Australopithecine ancestors who lived around three million years ago. They had just left the forest and moved to the savanna where their upright posture helped to see longer distances for scavenging food and watching for predators. Compelled by the wild and threatful surroundings, once they started to live in groups, they required further social skills in order to manage their social relationships, which in turn proved to be an important trigger for the increase in the brain size. By developing social skills the Australopithecines formed alliances and coalitions within the group in order to supervise their survival inside their society as well as outside of it.

With the limited cranial capacity of about 500 cc, the Australopithecines did indeed encounter the dawn of modern human consciousness. They developed a kind of emotional communication, which was confined to physical gestures and primitive vocalization. But the problem was that any negative emotional outbreak could disrupt harmony in the group, causing a lot of noises, which would attract attention of the predators.

Naturally, this created an adaptive pressure on the species for cortical control of emotion and for the basic social emotions of sympathy, guilt, and shame which promote cohesiveness. This triggered an increase in the brain size which was mostly in the neocortex that added an extra layer to the whole brain and made room for more neurons. Thus, out of a growing need to survive in a social environment emerged the cortical control of limbic emotional responses.

The limbic system constructs all the emotional elements of your mental universe, which are then imposed on your conscious mind after passing through the cortical gateway of moderation under the watch of the Prefrontal Cortex in the Frontal Lobes of the Cerebral Cortex. This means, one may elicit typically racist responses at a subconscious level, triggered by outgroup stimulus, but if the vital force of conscience runs pure on the surface of consciousness, such primitive responses have no power in them to manifest through behavior. It is much easier to be a racist, a misogynist, a xenophobe, a homophobe, an islamophobe, than to be a conscientious and civilized human being. It takes a lot of internal efforts to break free from all the sociologically imposed prejudices and rise as a genuine human.

CHAPTER III
One Humanity

It is indeed very grand to conquer the external nature, but grander still is to conquer our internal nature. It is fantastic to know the laws that govern the external universe, but it is infinitely more fantastic still to know the laws that govern the ambitions, the passions, the sentiments and the will of humankind's internal universe. And thus, shall rise the conscience of thinking humanity above the primordial nature of prejudices and barbarianism.

Only fools neglect the living God – the Human Self, while running after imaginary shadows. Break all imaginations my friend – break all the shackles of worthless indoctrination that do more harm than good to whole humanity –

and rise. Rise from the ashes of primitive fanaticism and worthless bigotry. Break all imaginations – break all delusions – and let the light of one all-pervading humanism prevail from the North Pole to the South. The greatest misfortune that has befallen the world is that humanity has forgotten the innate natural characteristic of humanism, and has accepted all other man-made labels of differentiations as primary and irrefutable part of human existence. Now, you are the one who has to tear apart that misfortune with your own rational footsteps towards one humanity. You have one identity over everything else, it is that you are human. That's all that is necessary to progress – that's all that is necessary to live and let live.

The world needs something from you, my friend. It needs the heart that is deep as the ocean and infinite as the outer-space. Can you provide that my friend! Can you make your will so large and your conscience so sharp that in front of which, a thousand Everests and a thousand Kilimanjaros would bow! Call up the ever-pure, the effulgent and the ever-radiant character of true humanism in yourself and in others, and no racism shall have the power to thrive in such society even for a few seconds. You may be James the American, or Mary the British, or anything else, but before all that, you are a human. Mark you, human you are, and your religion, humanism.

Be pure, live a conscientious life, defend your dignity and be loving to others. Be gentle, but do not hesitate to be firm when the situation requires it. Remember, one who knows, what he knows and what he does not know, is a genius – a true sage. Such should be the character of a human in the thinking society. But keep in mind, the road towards the manifestation of such character is not easy. All great achievements are attained through mighty obstacles. Sacrifice everything you have, to build that character. Sacrifice everything that is yours, to call up the humans in others.

Lions, lions and lions – these are what the world needs. Vigorous, self-believing, young lion-hearts are wanted. Ten courageous brave-hearts in every nation shall be enough to rekindle the spark of one humanism in the whole world.

Become self-aware my friend! That's all you need, to proceed. As you become aware of your truest self, you will slowly come to learn that nothing in the universe can have power over you unless you allow it to exercise such a power. Nothing in the universe can have the power over the human self, until the self becomes a fool and loses independence. Due to the lack of self-awareness, the mind puts itself in a position of slavery of external forces. And it is only the mind that can free itself from all slavery. Set the mind free my friend, and it will find its own salvation! Set the Self free, and it will attain its own independence! Liberty of thought and the courage to act upon it, are the core principles of human existence – these are the principles of growth and wellbeing.

Remember there is no God other than the Self – and even if there is, it would be way beyond the puny human capacity of comprehension.

Hence, pay more attention to the Human Self than anything else, and feed it love, courage, and conscience – and you shall see, that all the barbarianism, bigotry and superstitions shall begin to fade away in front of its ever-glowing radiance.

O my mighty sisters and brothers, forget not that the ideal of humanity is the search of truth. In this pursuit, countless souls have sacrificed themselves in the past. And in this pursuit, countless more shall need to sacrifice themselves. This pursuit of truth – this pursuit of liberation, does not care about anything else but the values that the human heart is filled with. These values have defined our present – and these values shall define our future.

Be possessed, not with the evils of selfishness and bigotry, but with the values and vigor of humanism. Be possessed with courage. Be possessed with conscience. Be possessed with the power of reasoning. And above all, be possessed with tremendous confidence in the self. Remember this, there is no such thing as over-confidence. When someone deems you as over-confident, it simply reflects their own poverty of confidence.

If poverty defines greatness, then become the poorest person on earth, in terms of weakness and bigotry. And if wealth defines glory, then become the wealthiest person on earth, in terms of courage, confidence and reasoning. These three will be given to you by no one. You will have to manifest them within yourself by the efforts of your own. Remember, all the power you need, is born with you. You simply need to recognize it and then expand it to exponential proportions. Mark you, know thy self, and the world will be thy oyster!

Come my friend! Come out from the narrow lanes of selfishness, superstition and mysticism. Come out into the light of knowledge – into the light of wisdom – into the light of conscience! And with that glorious light shining bright in your hearts, let us all work together to make this whole world a sweet land of liberty – a land where the race that shall receive preference over everything else, is the human race – the religion that shall receive preference over everything else, is humanism – the God that shall receive preference over everything else, is the Human.

They say, love God, for it is the greatest virtue. I say, love humans, for there is no greater virtue, no greater religion, than the love of humanity. They say have faith in God, and God shall give you everything. I say, no God has the slightest power to give you anything, unless you have faith in yourself and you are prepared to act upon that faith. Faith in God is optional, what the world needs is faith in the Self, it needs faith in the Humans. A few thousand humans fired with the zeal of humanism, fortified with the eternal faith in the Self, and self-adorned with lion's courage, who can go over the length and breadth of the earth, preaching the gospel of humanism, the gospel of compassion, the gospel of reasoning, the gospel of one humanity, would suffice to humanize the whole world. These patriotic souls of Mother Earth would be enough to take the whole species forward. And it all begins with you.

Arise O lion-heart! Awake, O great soldier! Misery has come upon the world. It is wailing for help. It is wailing for redemption. Won't you do anything, my friend! Don't you feel your heart burning seeing all the pain around! Won't you devote yourself to the redemption of your own kind! How can you sleep so sound amidst this great turmoil! Rouse yourself my friend! Rouse all others! Don't be fearless, but tame your fears, and stop at nothing. Work, Work and work, until you either succeed in your mission, or you die! It is better to die as a lion, than to live as a sheep.

BIBLIOGRAPHY

Alemseged, Z., Spoor, F., Kimbel, W.H., Bobe, R., Geraads, D., Reed, D., Wynn, J.G., 2006. A juvenile early hominin skeleton from Dikika, Ethiopia. Nature 443, 296-30.

Amodio, D.M., & Devine, P.G. (2006). Stereotyping and evaluation in implicit race bias: Evidence for independent constructs and unique effects on behavior. Journal of Personality and Social Psychology, 91, 652-661. doi:10.1037/0022-3514.91.4.652

Anton, S. C. Natural history of Homo erectus. American Journal of Physical Anthropology S37, 126-70 (2003)

Asfaw, B., White, T., Lovejoy, O., Latimer, B., Simpson, S., Suwa, G., 1999. Australopithecus garhi: a new species of early hominid from Ethiopia. Science 284, 629-635.

Antón, S.C., 2003. Natural history of Homo erectus. Yearbook of Physical Anthropology 46, 126–170.

Armstrong E (1982) Mosaic evolution in the primate brain: differences and similarities in the hominoid thalamus. In: Armstrong E, Falk D (eds) Primate brain evolution: methods and concepts. Plenum, New York, pp 131–162

Baars, B. (1988), A Cognitive Theory of Consciousness (New York: Cambridge University Press).

Bancaud, J., Brunet-Bourgin, F., Chauvel, P. & Halgren, E. (1994), 'Anatomical origin of deja vu and vivid ''memories'' in human temporal lobe epilepsy', Brain, 117, pp. 71–90.

Baldo, J. V., Shimamura, A. P., Delis, D. C., Kramer, J., & Kaplan, E. (2001). Verbal and design fluency in patients with frontal lobe lesions. Journal of the International Neuropsychological Society, 7, 586–596.

Barbey, A. K., Colom, R., Solomon, J., Krueger, F., Forbes, C., & Grafman, J. (2012). An integrative architecture for general intelligence and executive function revealed by lesion mapping. Brain, 135, 1154–1164.

Barbey, A. K., Grafman, J. in press a. The prefrontal cortex and goal-directed social behavior. In J. Decety & J. Cacioppo (Eds.), The Handbook of Social Neuroscience. Oxford University Press.

Barbey, A. K., Koenigs, M., & Grafman, J. Dorsolateral prefrontal contributions to human working memory. Cortex, in press b.

Barbey, A. K., & Grafman, J. (2011). An integrative cognitive neuroscience theory for social reasoning and moral judgment. Wiley Interdisciplinary Reviews: Cognitive Science, 2, 55–67.

Basso, A., De Renzi, E., Faglioni, P., Scotti, G., & Spinnler, H. (1973). Neuropsychological evidence for the existence of cerebral areas critical to the performance of intelligence tasks. Brain, 96, 715–728.

Bechara, A., Damasio, A. R., Damasio, H., & Anderson, S. W. (1994). Insensitivity to future consequences following damage to human prefrontal cortex. Cognition, 50, 7–15.

Black, F. W. (1976). Cognitive deficits in patients with unilateral war-related frontal lobe lesions. Journal of Clinical Psychology, 32, 366–372.

Blair, C. (2006). How similar are fluid cognition and general intelligence? A developmental neuroscience perspective on fluid cognition as an aspect of human cognitive ability. Behavioral and Brain Sciences, 29, 109–125.

Blair, R. J. R., & Cipolotti, L. (2000). Impaired social response reversal: a case of "acquired sociopathy". Brain, 123, 1122–1141.

Bugg, J. M., Zook, N. A., DeLosh, E. L., Davalos, D. B., & Davis, H. P. (2006). Age differences in fluid intelligence: contributions of general slowing and frontal decline. Brain and Cognition, 62, 9–16.

Burgess, P. W., & Shallice, T. (1996). Response suppression, initiation and strategy use following frontal lobe lesions. Neuropsychologia, 34, 263–272.

Bear, D.M. (1979), 'Personality changes associated with neurologic lesions', in Textbook of Outpatient Psychiatry, ed. A. Lazare (Baltimore, MD: Williams and Wilkins Co.).

Bogen,J.E.(1995a), 'On the neurophysiology of consciousness: Part I. An overview', Consciousness and Cognition, 4, pp. 52–62.

Bogen, J.E. (1995b), 'On the neurophysiology of consciousness: Part II. Constraining the semantic prob- lem', Consciousness and Cognition, 4, pp. 137–58.

Buxhoeveden DP, Switala AE, Litaker M, Roy E, Casanova MF (2001) Lateralization of minicolumns in human planum temporale is absent in nonhuman primate cortex. Brain Behav Evol 57:349–358

Bregman, A. (1981), 'Asking the "what for" question', in Perceptual Organization, ed. M. Kubovy & J. Pomerantz (Hillsdale, NJ: Lawrence Erlbaum Associates).

Blumenschine, R. J. et al. Late Pliocene Homo and hominid land use from Western Olduvai Gorge, Tanzania. Science 299, 1217-12121 (2003)

Brunet ,M., Guy, F., Pilbeam,. D., Mackaye, H.T., Likius, A., Ahounta, D., Beauvilain, A., Blondel, C., Bocherens, H., Boisserie, J.R., De Bonis, L., Coppens, Y., Dejax, J., Denys, C., Duringer, P., Eisenmann, V.R., Fanone, G., Fronty, P., Geraads, D., Lehmann, T., Lihoreau, F., Louchart, A., Mahamat, A., Merceron, G., Mouchelin, G., Otero, O., Campomanes, P.P., De Leon, M.P., Rage, J.C., Sapanet, M., Schuster, M., Sudre, J., Tassy, P., Valentin, X., Vignaud, P., Viriot, L., Zazzo, A., Zollikofer, C., 2002. A new hominid from the Upper Miocene of

Chad, central Africa. Nature 418(6894), 145-151

Brunet, M., Guy, F., Pilbeam, D., Lieberman, D.E., Likius, A., Mackaye, H.T., de Leon, M.S.P., Zollikofer, C.P.E., Vignaud, P., 2005. New material of the earliest hominid from the Upper Miocene of Chad. Nature 434(7034), 752-755.

Berger, L.R., Clarke, R.J., 1995. Eagle involvement of the Taung child fauna. Journal of Human Evolution 29, 275-299.

Berger, T., Trinkaus, E., 1995. Patterns of trauma among the Neandertals. Journal of Archaeological Science 22, 841-852.

Berger, L.R., de Ruiter, D.J., Churchill, S.E., Schmid, P., Carlson, K.J., Dirks, P.H.G.M., Kibii, J.M., 2010. Australopithecus sediba: A New Species of Homo-Like Australopith from South Africa. Science 328, 195-204.

Bickerton, D. (2009). Adam's tongue: How humans made language and how language made humans. New York: Hill and Wang. Brothers, L. (2002). The social brain: A project for integrating primate behavior and neurophysiology in a new domain. In J. T. Cacioppo et al. (Eds.), Foundations in neuroscience, pp. 367. Cambridge, MA: MIT Press.

Balter, M., 2010. Candidate human ancestor from South Africa sparks praise and debate. Science 328, 154-155.

Bobe, R., Behrensmeyer, A.K., 2004. The expansion of grassland systems in Africa in relation to mammalian evolution and the origin of the genus Homo. Palaeogeography, Palaeoclimatology, Palaeoecology 207, 399-420.

Bolton, E.B. (1935) 'Effect of knowledge upon attitudes towards the negro', J.Soc.Psy. 6, 68–90.

Bolton, E.B. (1937) 'Measuring specific attitudes toward the social rights of the negro', J.Ab.Soc.Psy. 31,384–97.

Boring, E.G. (1942) Sensation and Perception in the History of Experimental Psychology, NY: AppletonCentury-Crofts.

Boring, E.G. (1950 [1929]) A History of Experimental Psychology, 2nd edn, NY: AppletonCenturyCrofts.

Bowler, P. (1983) The Eclipse of Darwinism, Baltimore and London: Johns Hopkins UP.

Boyd, W.C. and Boyd, L.G. (1937) 'Sexual and racial variation in ability to taste phenylthio-carbamide with some data on inheritance', Ann.Eug. 846–51.

Bradley, R.N. (1926) Racial Origins of English Character with an Appendix on Language, London: Allen & Unwin.

Brazziel, W.F. (1969) 'Letter from the South', Harvard Educational Review 3 (2), 348–56 (rep. Harvard Educational Review (1969) 200–8).

Brenman, M. (1940a) 'Minority group membership and religious, psychosexual, and social patterns in a group of middle-class Negro girls',J. Soc.Psy. 12,179–96.

Brenman, M. (1940b) 'The relationship between minority group membership and group identification in a group of urban middle-class Negro girls' , J.Soc.Psy. 11,171–97.

Brenner, A.B. (1948) 'Some psychoanalytic speculations on anti-semitism', The Psychoanalytic Review, 35 (1), 20–32.

Brigham, C.C. (1923) A Study of American Intelligence, Princeton: Princeton UP.

Brigham, C.C. (1930) 'Intelligence tests of immigrant groups' Psy.Rev. 37, 158–65.

Brinton, D.G. (1901) Races and Peoples, Philadelphia: McKay.

Brinton, D.G. (1902) The Basis of Social Relations. A Study in Ethnic Psychology, NY and London: Albermale.

Brody, N. (1992) Intelligence, 2nd edn, San Diego: Academic Press. Brown, P. (ed.) (1973) Radical Psychology, London: Tavistock.

Brown, R. (1958) Words and Things: An Introduction to Language, NY: Free Press.

Brown, W.O. (1934) 'Culture contact and race conflict', in E.B.Reuter (ed) (1934), 34–37.

Bruce, M. (1940) 'Factors affecting intelligence test performance of whites and Negroes in the rural South', Arch.Psy. 252,99

Clarke, R.J., Tobias, P.V., 1995. Sterkfontein Member 2 foot bones of the oldest South African hominid. Science 269, 521–524.

Churchland, P.S. (1986), Neurophilosophy (Cambridge, MA: The MIT Press). Churchland, P.S. (1996), 'The hornswoggle problem', Journal of Consciousness Studies, 3 (5–6), pp. 402–8.

Churchland, P.S. & Ramachandran, V.S. (1993), 'Filling in: Why Dennett is wrong', in Dennett and His Critics: Demystifying Mind, ed. B. Dahlbom (Oxford: Blackwell Scientific Press).

Churchland, P.S., Ramachandran, V.S. & Sejnowski, T.J. (1994), 'A critique of pure vision', in Large- scale Neuronal Theories of the Brain, ed. C. Koch & J.L. Davis (Cambridge, MA: The MIT Press).

Cicurel, R., "L'ordinateur ne digérera pas le cerveau", Sarina Editions, 2013

Cobb S., Ramachandran, V.S. & Hirstein, W. (in preparation), 'Evoked potentials during synesthesia'. Cohen, M.S., Kosslyn, S.M., Breiter, H.C. et al. (1996), 'Changes in cortical activity during mental rotation. A mapping study using functional MRI', Brain, 119, pp. 89–100.

Cozolino, L. (2006). The Neuroscience of Human Relationships and the Developing Brain. New York: W.W. Norton & Company.

Cohen, E. (1939) 'Cultural and personality factors in the attitudes of Russian Jewish clients toward relief' , Smith.Coll.Stud.S.W. 10, 151–2.

Cohen, P. (1992) '"It's racism what dunnit": hidden narratives in theories of racism', in J.Donald and A.Rattansi (eds) (1992), 62–103.

Comer, J.P. (1972 [1969]) 'White racism: its root, form and content', in R.L.Jones (ed.) (1972) 311–17.

Conklin, E.G. (1921) The Direction of Human Evolution, NY: Scribner's.

Connolly, J. (1994) 'Of race and right', Irish Times, 6 December.

Cook, S.W. (1957) 'Desegregation: a psychological analysis', Am.Psy. 12,1–13.

Coombe, V. and Little, A. (1986) Race and Social Work. A Guide to Training, London: Routledge.

Coon, C.S. (1963 [1962]) The Origin of Races, London: Jonathan Cape.

Costall, A. (1991) 'Frederic Bartlett and the rise of prehistoric psychology' in A.Still and A.Costa1 : (eds) Against Cognitivism: Alternative Foundations for Cognitive Psychology, Hemel Hempstead: Harvester-Wheatsheaf, 39–54.

Costall, A. (1992) 'Why isn't British psychology social? Frederic Bartlett's promotion of the new academic discipline', Canadian Psychology 33, 633–9.

Costall, A. (1995) 'Sir Frederic Bartlett', The Psychologist 8 (7), 307–8.

Cox, O.C. (1970 [1948]) Caste, Class & Race. A Study in Social Dynamics, NY: Modern Reader.

Crafts, L.W., Schneirla, T.C., Robinson, E.E. and Gilbert, R.W. (eds) (1938) Recent Experiments in Psychology, NY and London: McGraw-Hill.

Crane, A.C. (1923) 'Race differences in inhibition', Arch.Psy. 9, 2–84.

Criswell, J.H. (1937) 'Racial cleavage in negro-white groups', Sociometry, 1, 81–9.

Criswell, J.H. (1939) 'A sociornetric study of race cleavage', Arch.Psy. 235.

Crookshank, F.G. (1931 [1924]) The Mongol in Our Midst. A study of man and his three faces, 3rd edn, London: Kegan Paul, Trench, Trübner.

Cross, W.E. (1980) 'Models of psychological nigrescence', in R.L.Jones (ed.) (1980) 81–98.

Cross, W.E. (1991) Shades of Black: Diversity in African American Identity, Madison, WI: University of Wisconsin Press.

Culwick, A.T. and G.M. (1935) 'Religious and economic sanctions in a Bantu tribe', B.J.Psy.26(2), 183–91.

Curtin, P.D. (1964) The Image of Africa: British Ideas and Action, 1780–1850, Madison, WI: University of Wisconsin Press.

Crick, F. (1994), The Astonishing Hypothesis: The Scientific Search for the Soul (New York: Simon and Schuster). Crick, F. (1996), 'Visual perception: rivalry and consciousness', Nature, 379, pp. 485–6.

Crick, F. & Koch, C. (1992), 'The problem of consciousness', Scientific American, 267, pp. 152–9.

Darwin, Charles. "On the origin of species by means of natural selection" (original edition, 1859).

Darwin, Charles. "The Descent of Man" (original edition, 1871).

Dawkins, R. "The Selfish Gene", Oxford University Press, 1976

Dawkins, R. "The Magic of Reality", Bantam Press, 2011

Dart, R.A. Australopithecus africanus: the southern ape-man of Africa. Nature 115, 195-199 (1925)

Davenport, C.B. (1929) 'Do races differ in mental capacity?', Psychological Abstracts 1, 70–89.

Davenport, C.B. and Steggerda, M. (1928) Race Crossing in Jamaica, Washington: Carnegie Institute, Publication 395.

Davies, S.P. (1930) Social Control of the Mentally Deficient, NY: Thomas Y.Crowell.

Davis, A. and Dollard, J. (1940) Children of Bondage, Washington, DC: American Council on Education.

Davis, D.B. (1966) The Problem of Slavery in Western Culture, Ithaca, NY: Cornell UP.

Davis, M. and Hughes, A.G. (1927) 'An investigation into the comparative intelligence and attainments of Jewish and non-Jewish schoolchildren', B.J.Psy. 18 (2), 134–46.

Davis, T.E. (1937) 'Some racial attitudes of negro college and grade school students', JNE 6,157– 65.

Dawson, G.E. (1900/1) 'Children's interest in the Bible', Ped.Sem. 7, 151–78.

Dearborn, W.F. and Long, H.H. (1934) 'The physical and mental abilities of the American negro: a critical survey', JNE 3, 530–47.

Delaney, L. (1972) 'The other bodies in the river', in R.L.Jones (ed.) (1972) 335–43.

Denney, D. (1992) Racism and Anti-Racism in Probation, London: Routledge.

Dennis, W. (1940a) 'Does culture appreciably affect patterns of infant behavior?', J.Soc.Psy. 12, 305–17.

Dennis, W. (1940b) 'Piaget's questions applied to Zuni and Navaho children', Psy.Bull. 37, 520.

Dennis, W. (1940c) The Hopi Child, NY:Appleton-Century.

Dennis, W. and Dennis, M.G. (1940) 'The effect of cradling practices upon the onset of walking in Hopi children', J.Genet.Psy. 56,77–86.

Dennis, W. and Russell, R.W. (1940) 'Piaget's questions applied to Zuni children', Child Dev. 11, 181–7.

Dennett, D.C. (1991), Consciousness Explained (Boston, MA: Little, Brown and Co.).

Devinsky, O., Feldmann, E., Burrowes, K. & Broomfield, E. (1989), 'Autoscopic phenomena with seizures', Archives of Neurology, 46, pp. 1080–8.

Devinsky, O., Morrell, MJ, Vogt, BA. (1995) 'Contribution of anterior cingulate cortex to behavior', Brain, 118, pp. 279–306.

Domínguez-Rodrigo, M., Pickering, T.R., Semaw, S., Rogers, M.J., 2005. Cutmarked bones from Pliocene archaeological sites at Gona, Afar, Ethiopia: Implications for the functions of the world's oldest stone tools. Journal of Human Evolution 48, 109-121.

Dirks, P.G.H.M, Kibii, J.M., Kuhn, B.F., Steininger, C., Churchill, S.E., Kramers, J.D., Pickering, R., Farber, D.L., Mériaux, A.-S., Herries, A.I.R, King, G.C.P., Berger, L.R., 2010. Geological setting and age of Australopithecus sediba from Southern Africa. Science 328, 205-208.

DeGiorgio, M. et al. Out of Africa: modern human origins special feature: explaining worldwide patterns of human genetic variation using a coalescent-based serial founder model of migration outward from Africa. PNAS USA 106, 16057-16062 (2009)

Delson, E., Harvati, K., 2006. Return of the last Neanderthal. Nature 443, 762-763.

Driberg, J.H. (1929) The Savage as He Really Is, London: Routledge.

Droba, D.D. (1932) 'Education and negro attitudes', Sociol.Soc.Res. 17, 137–41.

DuBois, W.E.B. (1911a) Common Schools and the Negro American, Atlanta: Atlanta UP.

DuBois, W.E.B. (1911b) 'The Negro race in the U.S.A.', in G.Spiller (ed.) (1911), 348–64.

Dummet, A. (1973) A Portrait of English Racism, Harmondsworth: Penguin.

Dunlap, J.W. (1930) 'Race differences in the organization of numerical and verbal abilities', Arch.Psy. 19, 7–71.

Dubois, E.,. 1894. Pithecanthropus erectus: eine menschenaehnlich Uebergangsform aus Java. Batavia: Landsdrukerei.

Edelman, G. M. (1992). Bright air, brilliant fire: On the matter of the mind. New York: Basic Books.

Enard W, Przeworski M, Fisher SE, Lai CS, Wiebe V, Kitano T, Monaco AP, Pääbo S (2002) Molecular evolution of FOXP2, a gene involved in speech and language. Nature 418:869–872

Erikson, E.H. (1939) 'Observations on Sioux education', J.Psy. 7, 101–56.

Erikson, E.H. (1950) Childhood and Society, Harmondsworth: Penguin.

Estabrooks, G.H. (1928a) 'The enigma of racial intelligence', J.Genet.Psy. 35, 137–9.

Estabrooks, G.H. (1928b) 'That question of racial inferiority', Am.Anth. 30, 470–5.

Eugenics Society (1934) 'Aims and Objectives of the Eugenics Society', Eug.Rev. 26.

Evans Pritchard, E.E. (1937) Witchcraft, Oracles and Magic Among the Azande, Oxford: Clarendon Press.

Evarts, A.B. (1913) 'Dementia praecox in the colored race', Psychoanalytic Review 1, 388–403.

Evarts, A.B. (1916) 'The ontogenetic against the phylogenetic elements in the psychoses of the colored race', Psychoanalytic Review 3, 272–87.

Eysenck, H.J. (1954) Psychology of Politics, London: RKP.

Eysenck, H.J. (1957) Sense and Nonsense in Psychology, Harmondsworth: Penguin.

Eysenck, H.J. (1971) Race, Intelligence and Education, London: Temple Smith.

Eysenck, H.J. vs. Kamin, L. (1981) Intelligence: The Battle for the Mind, London: Pan.

Falk, D. et al. Early hominid brain evolution: a new look at old endocasts. Journal of Human Evolution 38, 695-717 (2000)

Farah, M.J. (1989), 'The neural basis of mental imagery', Trends in Neurosciences, 10, pp. 395–9.

Fiorini, M., Rosa, M.G.P., Gattass, R. & Rocha-Miranda, C.E. (1992), 'Dynamic surrounds of receptive fields in primate striate cortex: A physiological basis', Proceedings of the National Academy of Science 89, pp. 8547–51.

Fodor, J.A. (1975), The Language of Thought (Cambridge, MA: Harvard University Press). Frith, C.D. & Dolan, R.J. (1997), 'Abnormal beliefs: Delusions and memory', Paper presented at the May, 1997, Harvard Conference on Memory and Belief.

Finlay BL, Darlington RB (1995) Linked regularities in the development and evolution of mammalian brains. Science 268:1578–1584

Gazzaniga, M. S. (1985). The social brain. New York: Basic Books. Greenspan, S. I. and S. G. Shanker (2004). The first idea: How symbols, language, and intelligence evolved from our early primate ancestors to modern humans. Cambridge, MA: Da Capo Press.

Gazzaniga, M.S. (1993), 'Brain mechanisms and conscious experience', Ciba Foundation Symposium, 174, pp. 247–57. Gloor, P., Olivier, A., Quesney, L.F., Andermann, F., Horowitz, S. (1982), 'The role of the limbic system in experiential phenomena of temporal lobe epilepsy', Annals of Neurology, 12, pp. 129–43.

Gloor, P. (1992), 'Amygdala and temporal lobe epilepsy', in The Amygdala: Neurobiological Aspects of Emotion, Memory and Mental Dysfunction, ed J.P. Aggleton (New York: Wiley-Liss).

Goodman M, Grossman LI, Wildman DE (2005) Moving primate genomics beyond the chimpanzee genome. Trends Genet 21:511–517

Goldberg, G., Mayer, N. & Toglis, J.U. (1981), 'Medial frontal cortex and the alien hand sign', Archives of Neurology, 38, pp. 683–6.

Grady, D. (1993), 'The vision thing: Mainly in the brain', Discover, June, pp. 57–66.

Green, R.E. A draft sequence of the Neandertal genome. Science 328, 710-722

Gilbert SL, Dobyns WB, Lahn BT (2005) Genetic links between brain development and brain evolution. Nat Rev Genet 6:581–590

Halgren, E. (1992), 'Emotional neurophysiology of the amygdala within the context of human cognition', in The Amygdala: Neurobiological Aspects of Emotion, Memory and Mental Dysfunction, ed J.P. Aggleton (New York: Wiley-Liss).

Harcourt-Smith, W. E. & L.C. Aiello. Fossils, feet and the evolution of human bipedal locomotion. Journal of Anatomy 204, 403-416 (2004)

Hartley, C.A. & Phelps, E.A. Changing fear: the neurocircuitry of emotion regulation. Neuropsychopharmacology 35, 136–146 (2010).

Haile-Selassie, Y., Suwa, G., White, T.D., 2004. Late Miocene teeth from Middle Awash, Ethiopia, and early hominid dental evolution. Science 303, 1503-1505.

Horgan, J. (1994), 'Can science explain consciousness?', Scientific American, 271, pp. 88–94.

Humphrey, N. (1993), A History of the Mind (London: Vintage).

Hublin, J.J. The origin of Neanderthals. PNAS 45, 169-177 (2009)

Henshilwood, C.S., Marean, C.W., 2003. The origin of modern human behavior: critique of the models and their test implications. Current Anthropology 44, 627-651.

Hof PR, Nimchinsky EA, Perl DP, Erwin JM (2001) An unusual population of pyramidal neurons in the anterior cingulate cortex of hominids contains the calcium- binding protein calretinin. Neurosci Lett 307:139–142

Hilton, C.E. (Eds) From Biped to Strider: The Emergence of Modern Human Walking, Running, and Resource Transport. Kluwer Academic/Plenum, New York, pp 50-52.

Haeusler, M., McHenry, H., 2004. Body proportions of Homo habilis reviewed. Journal of Human Evolution 46, 433-465.

Hobbs, J. (2006). The origins and evolution of language: A plausible strong-AI account. In M. Arbibi (Ed.), Action to language via the mirror neuron system. Cambridge: Cambridge University Press.

Holloway RL, Broadfield DC, Yuan MS (2004) The human fossil record, vol 3, Brain endocasts: the paleo- neurological evidence. Wiley, New York

Holloway RL (1996) Evolution of the human brain. In: Lock A, Peters CR (eds) Handbook of human symbolic evolution. Oxford University Press, Oxford, pp 74–114

Horowitz, E.L. (1935) 'A study of the process of the development of attitudes toward negroes', Psy.Bull. 32, 575–6.

Horowitz, E.L. (1936) 'The development of attitude toward the Negro', Arch.Psy. 194.

Horowitz, E.L. (1944) '"Race" attitudes', in O.Klineberg(ed.) (1944), 139–247.

Horowitz, R.E. (1939) 'Racial aspects of self-identification in nursery school children' J.Psy. 7, 91– 9.

Hose, C. and McDougall, W. (1912) The Pagan Tribes of Borneo, a Description of their Physical, Moral, and Intellectual Condition with Some Discussion of their Ethnic Relations, 2 vols, London: Macmillan.

Houts, P.L. (ed.) (1977) The Myth ofMeasurability, NY: Hart.

Howard, J.H. (1972) 'Toward a social psychology of colonialism', in R.L.Jones (ed.) (1972), 326– 34.

Howe, M. (1988) 'Intelligence as an explanation', B J.Psy. 79 (3), 349–60.

Howitt, D. (1993) 'Racist psychology where?', The Psychologist 6 (5), 202–3.

Howitt, D. and Owusu-Bempah, J. (1994) The Racism of Psychology: Time for a Change, Hemel Hempstead: Harvester-Wheatsheaf.

Hudson, W. (1960) 'Pictorial depth-perception in sub-cultural groups in Africa', J.Soc.Psy. 52, 183– 208.

Hudson, W. (1967) 'The study of the problem of pictorial perception among unacculturated groups', International Journal of Psychology 2, 90–107 (rep. in D.R.Price-Williams (ed.) 1969, 132–60).

Hughes, A.G. (1928) 'Jews and Gentiles. Their intellectual and temperamental differences', Eug.Rev. 20, 89–97.

Humphrey, S.K. (1917) Mankind: Racial Values and the Racial Prospect, NY: Scribner's.

Hunt, J. (1863) 'On the Negro's place in nature', Memoirs Read before the Anthropological Society of London 1, 1–64.

Hurlock, E.B. (1927) 'Color preferences of white and negro children', J.Comp.Psy. 7, 389–04.

Hurlock, E.B. (1930) 'The will-temperament of white and negro children', J.Genet.Psy. 38, 91– 100.

Huxley, J. (1936) 'Galton lecture: eugenics and society', Eug.Rev. 28, 11–31.

Huxley, J. and Haddon, A.C. (1935) We Europeans, London: Cape.

Jackson, T.S. (1940) 'Racial inferiority among negro children', Crisis 47, 241–66.

Johanson, D.C., White, T.D., Coppens, Y. 1978. A new species of the genus Australopithecus (Primates: Hominidae) from the Pliocene of Eastern Africa. Kirtlandia 28, 2-14.

Johanson, D.C., Edey, M.E., 1981. Lucy: The Beginnings of Humankind. St Albans, Granada.

Jackendoff, R. (1987), Consciousness and the Computational Mind (Cambridge, MA: The MIT Press).

Kanizsa, G. (1979), Organization In Vision (New York: Praeger).

Kanwisher, N., McDermott, J. & Chun, M.M. The fusiform face area: a module in human extrastriate cortex specialized for the perception of faces. J. Neurosci. 17, 4302–4311 (1997).

Kuypers HGJM (1958) Corticobulbar connections to the pons and lower brainstem in man. Brain 81:364–388

Kinsbourne, M. (1995), 'The intralaminar thalamic nucleii', Consciousness and Cognition, 4, pp. 167–71.

Kimbel, W.H., Delezene, L.K., 2009. "Lucy" redux: A review of research on

Australopithecus afarensis. Yearbook of Physical Anthropology 52, 2-48.

Kimbel, W. H. et al. Systematic assessment of a maxilla of Homo from Hadar, Ethiopia. American Journal of Physical Anthropology 103, 235-262 (1997)

Kunimatsu, Y. et al. A new Late Miocene great ape from Kenya and its implications for the origins of African great apes and humans. PNAS USA 104, 19661-19662. (2007)

King, W., 1864. The reputed fossil man of the Neanderthal. Quarterly Review of Science 1, 88-97.

Lackner,J.R.(1988),'Someproprioceptiveinflu encesonperceptualrepresentations',Brain,11 1,pp.281–97.

Lakoff, G. and M. Johnson (1999). Philosophy in the flesh. Basic Books: New York. LeDoux, J. E. (1996). The emotional brain. New York: Simon & Schuster.

Lalueza-Fox, C., Römpler, H., Caramelli, D., Stäubert, C., Catalano, G., Hughes, D., Rohland, N., Pilli, E., Longo, L., Condemi, S., de la Rasilla, M., Fortea, J., Rosas, A., Stoneking, M., Schöneberg, T., Bertranpetit, J., Hofreiter, M., 2007. A Melanocortin 1 Receptor Allele Suggests Varying Pigmentation Among Neanderthals. Science 318, 1453-1455.

Lacruz, R.S., Rozzi, F.R, Bromage, T.G., , 2005. Dental enamel hypoplasia, age at death, and weaning in the Taung child. South African Journal of Science 101, 567-569.

Le Gros Clark W.E., 1964. The fossil evidence for human evolution, 2nd ed. Chicago: University of Chicago Press. Leonard, W.R., Robertson, M.L., 1997.

Leakey, L.S.B., Tobias, P.V., Napier, J.R., 1964. A new species of the genus Homo from Olduvai Gorge. Nature 202, 7-9.

LeDoux, J.E. (1992), 'Emotion and the amygdala', in The Amygdala:

Neurobiological Aspects of Emo- tion, Memory and Mental Dysfunction, ed J.P. Aggleton (New York: Wiley-Liss).

Lieberman, M.D., Hariri, A., Jarcho, J.M., Eisenberger, N.I. & Bookheimer, S.Y. An fMRI investigation of race-related amygdala activity in African-American and Caucasian-American individuals. Nat. Neurosci. 8, 720–722 (2005).

Maryansky, A. (1996). African Ape social structure: A blue print for reconstructing early hominid structure. In J. Steel, S. Sherman (Eds.), The Archeology of Human Ancestry. London: Rutledge.

Massey, D. (2000). What I don't know about my field but wish I did. Annual Review of Sociology, 26(1), 699.

Massey, D. S. (2002). A brief history of human society: The origin and role of emotion in social life: 2001 presidential address. American Sociological Review, 67(1), 1–29.

Miller, B. D. (2007). Cultural anthropology, 4th ed. Boston: Allyn & Bacon.

Mayr, E., 1950. Taxonomic categories of fossil hominids. Cold Spring Harbor Symp Quant Biol 25, 109–118.

Martinez, I., Rosa, L., Arsuaga, J.-L. Jarabo, P., Quam, R., Lorenzo, C., Gracia, A., Carretero, J.-M., Bermúdez de Castro, J.M., Carbonell, E., 2004. Auditory capacities in Middle Pleistocene humans from the Sierra de Atapuerca in Spain. Proceedings of the National Academy of Sciences 101, 9976-9981.

Mounier, A., Marchal, F., Condemi, S. 2009. Is Homo heidelbergensis a distinct species? New insight on the Mauer mandible". Journal of Human Evolution 56, 219-246.

McHenry, H., 1998. Body proportions in Australopithecus afarensis and A. africanus and the origin of the genus Homo. Journal of Human Evolution 35, 1-22.

McHenry, H. M. Body size and proportions in early hominids. American Journal of Physical Anthropology 87, 407-431 (1992)

McBrearty, S., Brooks, A., 2000. The revolution that wasn't: a new interpretation of the origin of modern humans. Journal of Human Evolution 39, 453-563.

MacDonald, A.W., Cohen, J.D., Stenger, V.A. & Carter, C.S. Dissociating the role of the dorsolateral prefrontal and anterior cingulate cortex in cognitive control. Science 288, 1835–1838 (2000)

MacLean, P.D. (1990), The Triune Brain in Evolution (New York: Plenum Press).

MacKay, D.M. (1969), Information, Mechanism and Meaning (Cambridge, MA: The MIT Press).

Marr, D. (1982), Vision (San Francisco: Freeman). Medawar, P. (1969), Induction and Intuition in Scientific Thought (London: Methuen).

Milner, A.D. & Goodale, M.A. (1995), The Visual Brain In Action (Oxford: Oxford University Press).

Nagel, T. (1974), 'What is it like to be a bat?', Philosophical Review, 83, pp. 435–50.

Nash, M. (1995), 'Glimpses of the mind', Time, pp. 44–52.

Naskar, Abhijit. (2016), "What is Mind?"

Naskar, Abhijit. (2017), "The Education Decree"

Naskar, Abhijit. (2017), "Principia Humanitas"

Nicolelis, M. & Cicurel, R., "The Relativistic Brain: How it works and why it cannot be simulated by a Turing machine", Kioss Press, 2015

Nielson, J.M. & Jacobs, L.L. (1951), 'Bilateral lesions of the anterior cingulate gyri', Bulletin of the Los Angeles Neurological Society, 16, pp. 231–4.

Nimchinsky EA, Gilissen E, Allman JM, Perl DP, Erwin JM and Hof PR (1999) A neuronal morphologic type unique to humans and great apes. Proc Natl Acad Sci USA 96:5268–5273

Novembre, J., J. K. Pritchard and G. Coop (2007). Adaptive drool in the gene pool. Nature Genetics, 39, 1188.

O'Donnell, J.M. (1985) The Origins of Behaviorism: American Psychology, 1870–1920, NY and London: NYUP.

Penfield, W.P. & Perot, P. (1963), 'The brain's record of auditory and visual experience: a final summary and discussion', Brain, 86, pp. 595–696.

Penrose, R. (1994), Shadows of the Mind (Oxford: Oxford University Press).

Penrose, R. (1989), The Emperor's New Mind: Concerning Computers, Minds and The Laws of Physics (Oxford: Oxford University Press).

Phelps, E.A., Cannistraci, C.J. & Cunningham, W.A. Intact performance on an indirect measure of race bias following amygdala damage. Neuropsychologia 41, 203–208 (2003).

Plum, F. & Posner, J.B. (1980), The Diagnosis of Stupor and Coma (Philadelphia: F.A. Davis and Co.).

Posner, M.I. & Raichle, M.E. (1994), Frames of Mind (New York: Scientific American Library).

Preuss TM, Caceres M, Oldham MC, Geschwind DH (2004) Human brain evolution: insights from micro- arrays. Nat Rev Genet 5:850–860

Purpura K.P. & Schiff, N.D. (1997), 'The thalamic intralaminar nuclei: a role in visual awareness', The Neuroscientist, 3, pp. 8–15.

Pickford, M., Senut, B., 2001. 'Millennium Ancestor', a 6-million-year-old bipedal hominid from Kenya - Recent discoveries push back human origins by 1.5 million years. South African Journal of Science 97, 22-22.

Pickford, M., Senut, B., Gommery, D., Triel, J., 2002. Bipedalism in Orrorin tugenensis revealed by its femora. Comptes Rendus Palevol 1, 191-203.

Ramachandran, V.S. (1993), 'Filling in gaps in logic: Some comments on Dennett', Consciousness and Cognition, 2, pp. 165–8.

Ramachandran,V.S.(1995a),'Fillingingapsinl ogic:ReplytoDurginetal.',Perception, 24,pp.41-845.

Ramachandran, V.S. and Blakeslee, S. (1999), Phantoms in the Brain: Probing the Mysteries of the Human Mind (William Morrow Paperbacks)

Richmond, B.G., Jungers, W.L., 2008. Orrorin tugenensis femoral morphology and the evolution of hominin bipedalism. Science 319, 1662-1665.

Rilling JK Human and nonhuman primate brains: are they allometrically scaled versions of the same design? Evol Anthropol 15:65–77

Relethford, J. H. Genetic evidence and the modern human origins debate. Heredity 100, 555-563 (2008)

Rightmire, G. P. Out of Africa: modern human origins special feature: middle and later Pleistocene hominins in Africa and Southwest Asia. PNAS USA 106, 16046-16050 (2009)

Rightmire, G.P. Homo in the Middle Pleistocene: Hypodigms, variation, and species recognition. Evolutionary Anthropology 17, 8-21 (2008)

Roebroeks, W. & P. Villa. On the earliest evidence for habitual use of fire in Europe. PNAS USA Epub ahead of print (2011)

Rossion, B., Schiltz, C. & Crommelinck, M. The functionally defined right occipital and fusiform face areas discriminate novel from visually familiar face. Neuroimage 19, 877–883 (2003).

Roth, G. and Dicke, U. Evolution of the brain and intelligence, TRENDS in Cognitive Sciences Vol. 9, No. 5, 2005

Rightmire, G.P., 1998. Human evolution in the Middle Pleistocene: the role of Homo heidelbergensis. Evolutionary Anthropology 6, 218-227.

Searle, John R. (1980), 'Minds, brains, and programs', Behavioral and Brain Sciences, 3, pp. 417–58.

Searle, John R. (1992), The Rediscovery of the Mind (Cambridge, MA: The MIT Press).

Semendeferi K, Lu A, Schenker N, Damasio H (2002) Humans and great apes share a large frontal cortex. Nat Neurosci 5:272–276

Strauss, E., Risser, A. & Jones, M.W. (1982), 'Fear responses in patients with epilepsy', Archives of Neu- rology, 39, pp. 626–30.

Schoetensack, O., 1908. Der Unterkiefer des Homo heidelbergensis aus den Sanden von Mauer bei Heidelberg. Leipzig: Wilhelm Engelmann.

Stringer, C.B., Trinkaus, E., Roberts, M.B., Parfitt, S.A., Macphail, R.I., 1998.The Middle Pleistocene human tibia from Boxgrove. Journal of Human Evolution 34, 509-547.

Scott, R. S., Ungar, P.S., Bergstrom, T.S., Brown, C.A., Grine, F.E, Teaford, M.F., Walker, A., 2005. Dental microwear texture analysis shows within-species diet variability in fossil hominins. Nature 436, 693-695.

Schmid, P., 2004. Functional interpretation of the Laetoli footprints. In: Meldrum, D.J.,

Senut, B. et al. First hominid from the Miocene (Lukeino Formation, Kenya). C. R. Acad. Sci. Paris, Sciences de la Senut, B., Pickford, M., Gommery, D., Mein, P., Cheboi, K., Coppens, Y., 2001. First hominid from the Miocene (Lukeino Formation, Kenya). Comptes Rendus De L Academie Des Sciences Serie Ii Fascicule a-Sciences De La Terre Et Des Planetes 332, 137-144.

Sherwood CC, Broadfield DC,Gannon PJ,Holloway RL, Hof PR (2003) Variability of Brocas area homologue in African great apes: implications for language evolution. Anat Rec 71A:276–285

Smith, C.E. (1934) 'A new approach to the problem of racial differences', JNE 3, 523–9

Spoor, F., Leakey, M.G., Gathogo, P.N., Brown, F.H., Antón, S.C., McDougall, I., Kiarie, C. Manthi, F.K, Leakey, L.N., 2007. Implications of new early Homo fossils from Ileret, east of Lake Turkana, Kenya. Nature 448, 688–691.

Stringer, C.B., Finlayson, J.C., Barton, R.N.E, Fernández-Jalvo, Y., Cáceres, I., Sabin, R.C., Rhodes, E.J., Currant, A.P., Rodríguez-Vidal, J., Giles-Pacheco, F., Riquelme-Cantal, J.A., 2008. Neanderthal exploitation of marine mammals in Gibraltar. Proceedings of the National Academy of Sciences USA 105, 14319–14324.

Shipman, P., 2008. Separating "us" from "them": Neanderthal and modern human behavior. Proceedings of the National Academy of Sciences USA 105, 14241-14242.

Schmitt, D., Churchill, S., 2003. Experimental evidence concerning spear use in Neandertals and early modern humans. Journal of Archaeological Science 30, 103-114.

Sutherland, N.S. (1989), The International Dictionary of Psychology (New York: Continuum).

Sawer, G. and Deak, V. (2007). The last human (p. 103). New York: Peter N. Nevraumont Publication – Yale University Press.

Small, D. (2008). On the deep history of the brain. Berkeley: University of California Press.

Turner, B. (2000a). Embodied ethnography. Doing culture. Social Anthropology, 8(1), 51.

Turner, J. H. (2000b). On the origins of human emotions: A sociological inquiry into the evolution of human affect. Stanford, California: Stanford University Press.

Tovee, M.J., Rolls, E.T. & Ramachandran, V.S. (1996), 'Rapid visual learning in neurones of the primate temporal visual cortex', Neuroreport, 7, pp. 2757–60.

Trinkhaus, E., 1985. Pathology and the posture of the La Chappelle-aux-Saints Neanderthal. American Journal of Physical Anthropology 67, 19-41.

Trinkaus, E., Shipman, P., 1993. The Neanderthals: Changing the Image of Mankind. Knopf: New York.

Thorpe, S.K.S., Holder, R.L., Crompton, R.H., 2007. Origin of human bipedalism as an adaptation for locomotion on flexible branches. Science 316, 1328-1331.

Terre et des planètes / Earth and Planetary Sciences 332, 137-144 (2001)

Ungar, P.S., Grine, F.E., Teaford, M.F., El-Zaatari, S., 2006. Dental microwear and diets of African early Homo. Journal of Human Evoution 50, 78–95

Ungar, P.S., Grine, F.E., Teaford, M.F., 2006. Diet in early Homo: a review of the evidence and a new model of adaptive versatility. Annual Review of Anthropology 35, 209-228.

Waxman, S.G. & Geschwind, N. (1975), 'The interictal behavior syndrome of temporal lobe epilepsy', Archives of General Psychiatry, 32, pp. 1580-6.

Ward, C. V. et al. Complete fourth metatarsal and arches in the foot of Australopithecus afarensis. Science 331, 750-753 (2011)

Ward, C. V. Interpreting the posture and locomotion of Australopithecus afarensis: where do we stand? American Journal of Physical Anthropology S35, 185-215 (2002)

White, T. D. et al. Ardipithecus ramidus and the paleobiology of early hominids. Science 326, 75-86 (2009)

Wong, K., 2010. Spectacular South African skeletons reveal new species from murky period of human evolution. Scientific American 8 April 2010

Wong, K., 2010. Fossils of our family. Scientific American June 2010.

Woodworth, R.S. (1910a) 'Racial differences in mental traits', Science N.S. 31, 171–86.

Woodworth, R.S. (1910b) 'The puzzle of color vocabularies', Psy.Bull. 1 (10), 325–34.

Woodworth, R.S. (1916) 'Comparative psychology of races', Psy.Bull. 13, 388–96.

Woodworth, R.S. (1918) Dynamic Psychology. The Jessup Lectures 1916–1917, NY: Columbia UP.

Woodworth, R.S. (1946, 18th edn) Psychology. A Study of Mental Life, London: Methuen

Wray,A.(1998)."Protolanguage as a holistic system for social interaction," Language & Communication 18, pp. 47–67.

Young, N. M. et al. The phylogenetic position of Morotopithecus. Journal of Human Evolution 46, 163-184 (2004)

Zeki, S.M. (1978), 'Functional specialisation in the visual cortex of the rhesus monkey', Nature, 274, pp. 423–8.

Zeki, S.M. (1993), A Vision of the Brain (Oxford: Oxford University Press).

Zollikofer, C. P. et al. Virtual cranial reconstruction of Sahelanthropus tchadensis. Nature 434, 755-759 (2005)

WE ARE ALL BLACK

Made in the USA
Middletown, DE
31 January 2021

32808564R00109